FINANCIAL REPORT

THE NUMBERS

JOHN A. TRACY

Published by John Wiley & Sons, Inc., Hoboken, New Jersey.
Published simultaneously in Canada.

For general information on our other products and services or for technical support, please contact our Customer Care Department within the United States at (800) 762-2974, outside the United States at (317) 572-3993 or fax (317) 572-4002.

Wiley also publishes its books in a variety of electronic formats. Some content that appears in print may not be available in electronic books. For more information about Wiley products, visit our web site at www.wiley.com.

Library of Congress Cataloging-in-Publication Data

Tracy, John A.
  How to read a financial report : wringing vital signs out of the numbers / John A. Tracy. — 7th ed.
    p. cm.
  Includes bibliographical references and index.
  ISBN 978-0-470-40530-7 (pbk.)
    1. Financial statements. I. Title.
  HF5681.B2T733 2009
  657'.3—dc22

                                                              2008047055

Printed in the United States of America.

10 9 8 7 6 5 4 3 2 1

PREFACE TO THE SEVENTH EDITION

When I started this book, we had no grandchildren; we now have 12. At the time the first edition was released in 1980, the Dow Jones Industrial Average hovered around 850 (really!). This most-watched stock market index reached 11,700 in early 2000, and then it abruptly plunged, causing a big dent in my retirement savings. The Dow recovered over the following years, but then dropped again. As I write this sentence the Dow is on the north side of 8,000. As J. P. Morgan once said: "The market will fluctuate." Millions of individuals keep their money in the stock market, and stock investments are a large part of most retirement plans. Knowing how to read a financial report is as important as ever.

In the Preface to the sixth edition I spoke about the alarming surge of financial reporting frauds that culminated in the infamous Enron scandal, which brought down the venerable CPA firm Arthur Andersen. The fallout from these financial frauds was widespread and caused billions of dollars of losses to investors. The good news is that we have come a long way from those dismal days.

The federal legislation passed in response to the Enron debacle has been largely effective. Corporate executives and CPA auditors of public companies now operate under new rules. The general view is that the new rules governing financial reporting and auditing will make the stock market a fairer place to invest money. But we shouldn't let our guard down. The first defense is, as always, to have a clear-minded understanding of financial statements and the limits of financial reporting.

This edition catches up with the major changes in financial reporting and auditing since the previous edition. At the top of this list is the movement toward international financial reporting and accounting standards. At the same time, the basic architecture of the book remains unchanged. The framework of the book has proved very successful for more than 25 years. I'd be a fool to mess with this success formula. My mother did not raise a fool. Cash flows are underscored throughout the book. This cash flow emphasis is the hallmark of the book.

All the exhibits in this edition have been refreshed to make them clearer and crisper. I prepared these exhibits as Excel worksheets. To request a copy of the workbook file of all the exhibits, please contact me at my e-mail address: tracyj@colorado.edu. I'm retired now, so I have more time to read and answer my e-mails. I express my sincere thanks to all of you who have sent compliments about my book. The royalties from sales of the book are nice, but the bouquets from readers are icing on the cake.

Not many books of this ilk make it to the seventh edition. It takes a good working partnership between the author and the publisher. I thank most sincerely the many persons at John Wiley & Sons who have worked with me on the book for going on three decades now. The suggestions on my first draft of the book by Joe Ross, then national training director of Merrill Lynch, were extraordinarily helpful. The continuing support of Debra Englander, Executive Editor at Wiley, is much appreciated. And I'd be remiss without mentioning Mary Daniello and Kelly O'Connor, who have been such a pleasure to work with. Thanks go, too, to the staff at Cape Cod Compositors.

I dedicate this book to Gordon B. Laing, my original editor and sponsor of the book. His superb editing was a blessing that few authors enjoy. His guidance, encouragement, and enthusiasm made all the difference. He was a true gentleman who taught me a great deal about writing. His criticisms of my manuscript drafts were sharp but always kindly and supportive. Gordon took much pride in the success of the book—as well he should have! To my great sorrow Gordon died in early 2003. If somehow he can hear this message, I'd like to say again: Gordon, I couldn't have done it without you.

JOHN A. TRACY

Boulder, Colorado
March 2009

CONTENTS

HOW TO READ A FINANCIAL REPORT

Part One

COMPONENTS AND CONNECTIONS IN FINANCIAL STATEMENTS

1

STARTING WITH CASH FLOWS

Importance of Cash Flows: Cash Flows Summary for a Business

Business managers, lenders, and investors, quite rightly, focus on *cash flows*. Cash inflows and outflows are the heartbeat of every business. Without a steady heartbeat of cash flows, a business would soon die.

So, we'll start with cash flows. For our example I use a business that has been operating many years. This established business makes profit regularly and, equally important, it keeps in good financial condition. It has a good credit history, and banks lend money to the business on competitive terms. Its present share-owners would be willing to invest additional capital in the business, if needed. None of this comes easy. It takes good management to make profit consistently, to secure capital, and to stay out of financial trouble. Many businesses fail these imperatives.

Exhibit 1.1 summarizes the company's cash inflows and out-flows for the year just ended, and shows two separate groups of cash flows. First are the cash flows of its profit-making activities—cash inflows from sales and cash outflows for expenses. Second are the other cash inflows and outflows of the business—raising capital, investing capital in assets, and distributing some of its profit to shareowners.

I assume you're fairly familiar with the cash inflows and out-flows listed in Exhibit 1.1. Therefore, I'll be brief in describing the cash flows at this early point in the book:

- The business received $51,680,000 during the year from selling products to its customers. It should be no surprise that this is its largest source of cash inflow. Cash inflow from sales revenue is needed for paying expenses. During the year the company paid $34,760,000 for the products it sells to customers. And, it had sizable cash outflows for operating expenses, interest on its debt (borrowed money), and income tax. The net result of its profit-making activities is a $3,105,000 cash increase for the year—an extremely important number that managers, lenders, and investors watch closely.

- Moving on to the second group of cash flows during the year, the business increased the amount borrowed on notes payable by $625,000, and its stockholders invested an additional $175,000 in the business. Together these two external sources of capital provided $800,000, which is in addition to the internal $3,105,000 cash from its profit-making activities during the year. On the other side of the ledger, the business spent $3,625,000 for building improvements, for new machines and equipment, and for intangible assets. Finally, the business distributed $750,000 cash to its shareowners from profit.

- The net result of the cash inflows and outflows is a $470,000 cash decrease during the year. Don't jump to any conclusions yet; the net decrease in cash in and of itself is neither good nor bad. You need more information than just a summary of cash flows to come to any conclusions about the financial affairs of the business.

EXHIBIT 1.1—SUMMARY OF CASH FLOWS DURING YEAR

Dollar Amounts in Thousands

	Cash Inflow (Outflow)	Net Cash Increase (Decrease)
Profit-Making Activities		
From sales of products to customers, including some sales made last year	$ 51,680	
For acquiring products that were sold or are still being held for future sale	(34,760)	
For operating expenses, some of which were incurred last year	(11,630)	
For interest on short-term and long-term debt, some of which applies to last year	(520)	
For income tax, some of which was paid on last year's taxable income	(1,665)	$ 3,105
Other Sources and Uses of Cash		
From increasing amount borrowed on interest-bearing notes payable	$ 625	
From issuing additional capital stock (ownership shares) in the business	175	
For building improvements, new machines, new equipment, and intangible assets	(3,625)	
For distributions to stockholders from profit	(750)	(3,575)
Net cash change during year		$ (470)

What Does Cash Flows Summary NOT Tell You?

In Exhibit 1.1 we see that cash, the all-important lubricant of business activity, deceased $470,000 during the year. In other words, the total of cash outflows exceeded the total of cash inflows by this amount for the year. The cash decrease and the reasons for the decrease are very important information. The cash flows summary tells a very important part of the story of a business. But, cash flows do not tell the whole story. Business managers, investors in a business, business lenders, and many others need to know two other types of information about a business that are *not* reported in its cash flows summary.

The two most important types of information that a summary of cash flows does not tell you are:

1. The *profit* earned (or *loss* suffered) by the business for the period.

2. The *financial condition* of the business at the end of the period.

Now just a minute. Didn't we just see in Exhibit 1.1 that the net cash increase from sales revenue less expenses was $3,105,000 for the year? You may well ask: "Doesn't this cash increase equal the amount of profit earned for the year?" No, it doesn't. The net cash flow from profit-making operations during the year does not equal the amount of profit earned for the year. In fact, it's not unusual that these two numbers are very different.

Profit is an *accounting-determined* number that requires much more than simply keeping track of cash flows. The differences between using a checkbook to measure profit and using accounting methods to measure profit are explained in the following section. Hardly ever are cash flows during a period the correct amounts for measuring a company's sales revenue and expenses for that period. Summing up, profit cannot be determined from cash flows.

Furthermore, a summary of cash flows reveals virtually nothing about the *financial condition* of a business. Financial condition refers to the assets of the business matched against its liabilities at the end of the period. For example: How much cash does the company have in its checking account(s) at the end of the year? We can see that over the course of the year the business decreased its cash balance by $470,000. But we can't tell from Exhibit 1.1 the company's ending cash balance. And, more importantly, a cash flows summary does not report the amounts of assets and liabilities of the business at the end of the period.

Profit Cannot Be Measured by Cash Flows

The company in this example sells products on *credit*. The business offers its customers a short period of time to pay for their purchases. Most of the company's sales are to other businesses, which demand credit. (In contrast, most retailers selling to individuals accept credit cards instead of extending credit to their customers.) In this example the company collected $51,680,000 from its customers during the year. However, some of this cash inflow was for sales made in the *previous* year. And, some sales made on credit in the year just ended had not been collected by the end of the year.

At year-end the company had *receivables* from sales made to its customers during the latter part of the year. These receivables will be collected early next year. Because some cash was collected from last year's sales and some cash was not collected from sales made in the year just ended, the total amount of cash collections during the year does not equal the amount of *sales revenue* for the year.

Cash disbursements during the year are *not* the correct amounts for measuring expenses. The company paid $34,760,000 for products that are sold to customers (see Exhibit 1.1). At year-end, however, many products were still being held in *inventory*. These products had not yet been sold by year-end. Only the cost of products sold and delivered to customers during the year should be deducted as expense from sales revenue to measure profit. Don't you agree?

Furthermore, some of the company's product costs had not yet been paid by the end of the year. The company buys on credit the raw materials used in manufacturing its products and takes several weeks before paying its bills. The company has *liabilities* at year-end for recent raw material purchases and for other manufacturing costs as well.

There's more. Its cash payments during the year for operating expenses, as well as for interest and income tax expenses, are not the correct amounts to measure profit for the year. The company has liabilities at the end of the year for *unpaid expenses*. The cash outflow amounts shown in Exhibit 1.1 do not include the amounts of unpaid expenses at the end of the year.

In short, cash flows from sales revenue and for expenses are not the correct amounts for measuring profit for a period of time. Cash flows take place too late or too early for correctly measuring profit for a period. Correct timing is needed to record sales revenue and expenses in the right period.

The correct timing of recording sales revenue and expenses is called *accrual-basis accounting*. Accrual-basis accounting recognizes receivables from making sales on credit and recognizes liabilities for unpaid expenses in order to determine the correct profit measure for the period. Accrual-basis accounting also is necessary to determine the financial condition of a business—to record the assets and liabilities of the business.

Cash Flows Do Not Reveal Financial Condition

The cash flows summary for the year (Exhibit 1.1) does not reveal the financial condition of the company. Managers certainly need to know which assets the business owns and the amounts of each asset, including cash, receivables, inventory, and all other assets. Also, they need to know which liabilities the company owes and the amounts of each.

Business managers have the responsibility for keeping the company in a position to pay its liabilities when they come due to keep the business *solvent* (able to pay its liabilities on time). Furthermore, managers have to know whether assets are too large (or too small) relative to the sales volume of the business. Its lenders and investors want to know the same things about a business.

In brief, both the managers inside the business and lenders and investors outside the business need a summary of a company's financial condition (its assets and liabilities). Of course they need a profit performance report as well, which summarizes the company's sales revenue and expenses and its profit for the year.

A cash flows summary is very useful. In fact, a slightly different version of Exhibit 1.1 is one of the three primary financial statements reported by every business. But in no sense does the cash flows report take the place of the profit performance report and the financial condition report. The next chapter introduces these two financial statements, and shows the generally accepted format of a summary of cash flows (instead of the informal format shown in Exhibit 1.1).

A Final Note before Moving On: Over the past century (and longer) a recognized profession has developed, one of whose main functions is to prepare and report business financial statements—the *accounting profession*. In measuring profit and in reporting financial condition, businesses in the United States must follow established rules and standards that collectively are referred to as *generally accepted accounting principles* (GAAP). But, as I write this sentence, GAAP are undergoing dramatic changes. In later chapters I say a lot more about GAAP merging with international accounting and financial reporting standards.

2

THE THREE FINANCIAL STATEMENTS

Reporting Financial Condition, Profit Performance, and Cash Flows

Business managers, lenders, and investors need to know the financial condition of a business. They need a report that summarizes its assets and liabilities, as well as the ownership interests in the residual of assets over liabilities. And they need to know the profit performance of the business. They need a report that summarizes sales revenue and expenses for the most recent period and the resulting profit or loss. And, they need to know the cash flows of the business. Chapter 1 explains that a summary of cash flows, though very useful in its own right, does not provide information about the financial condition or the profit performance of a business.

Financial condition is communicated in an accounting report called the *balance sheet*, and profit performance is presented in an accounting report called the *income statement*. Cash flows are communicated in the *statement of cash flows*. Alternative titles for the balance sheet include "statement of financial condition" or "statement of financial position." An income statement may be titled "statement of operations" or "earnings statement." We'll stick with the names "balance sheet" and "income statement" to be consistent throughout the book.

The term "financial statements," in the plural, generally refers to a complete set that includes a balance sheet, an income statement, and a statement of cash flows. Informally, financial statements are called just "financials." In almost all cases the financial statements need to be supplemented with additional information, which is presented in *footnotes* and *supporting schedules*. The broader term "financial report" refers to all this, plus any additional narrative, graphics, and promotional content that accompany the financial statements and their footnotes and supporting schedules.

The three financial statements for the company example introduced in Chapter 1 are now presented in Exhibits 2.1, 2.2, and 2.3 on the following pages. The format and content of these three financial statements apply to manufacturers, wholesalers, and retailers—businesses that make or buy *products* that are sold to their customers. Although the financial statements of service businesses that don't sell products differ somewhat, Exhibits 2.1, 2.2, and 2.3 demonstrate the basic framework and content of balance sheets, income statements, and statements of cash flows for all businesses.

Side Notes: The term "profit" is mostly avoided in income statements. "Profit" comes across to many people as greedy or mercenary. The term suggests an excess or a surplus over and above what's necessary. You may hear business managers use the term "profit & loss" or "P&L statement" for the income statement. But this title hardly ever is used in external financial reports released outside a business.

Also, I should point out that most balance sheets do not include a column for changes as you see in Exhibit 2.1. However, we need these amounts in the following chapters.

EXHIBIT 2.1—YEAR-END BALANCE SHEET
Dollar Amounts in Thousands

	Last Year	This Year	Change		Last Year	This Year	Change
Cash	$ 3,735	$ 3,265	$ (470)	Accounts Payable	$ 2,675	$ 3,320	$ 645
Accounts Receivable	4,680	5,000	320	Accrued Expenses Payable	1,035	1,515	480
Inventory	7,515	8,450	935	Income Tax Payable	82	165	83
Prepaid Expenses	685	960	275	Short-Term Notes Payable	3,000	3,125	125
Current Assets	$16,615	$17,675		**Current Liabilities**	$ 6,792	$ 8,125	
Property, Plant, and Equipment	$13,450	$16,500	3,050	**Long-Term Notes Payable**	$ 3,750	$ 4,250	500
Accumulated Depreciation	(3,465)	(4,250)	(785)				
Cost Less Depreciation	$ 9,985	$12,250		Capital Stock—793,000 shares			
				and 800,000 shares respectively	$ 7,950	$ 8,125	175
Intangible Assets	$ 5,000	$ 5,575	575	Retained Earnings	13,108	15,000	1,892
Long-Term Operating Assets	$14,985	$17,825		**Stockholders' Equity**	$21,058	$23,125	
				Total Liabilities and			
Total Assets	$31,600	$35,500	$3,900	**Stockholders' Equity**	$31,600	$35,500	$3,900

EXHIBIT 2.2—INCOME STATEMENT FOR YEAR
Dollar Amounts in Thousands

Sales Revenue	$ 52,000
Cost of Goods Sold Expense	(33,800)
Gross Margin	$ 18,200
Selling, General, and Administrative Expenses	(12,480)
Depreciation Expense	(785)
Earnings before Interest and Income Tax	$ 4,935
Interest Expense	(545)
Earnings before Income Tax	$ 4,390
Income Tax Expense	(1,748)
Net Income	$ 2,642

EXHIBIT 2.3—STATEMENT OF CASH FLOWS FOR YEAR
Dollar Amounts in Thousands

Cash Flow from Operating Activities		
Net Income (from Income Statement)	$ 2,642	
Accounts Receivable Increase	(320)	
Inventory Increase	(935)	
Prepaid Expenses Increase	(275)	
Depreciation Expense	785	
Accounts Payable Increase	645	
Accrued Expenses Payable Increase	480	
Income Tax Payable Increase	83	$ 3,105
Cash Flow from Investing Activities		
Expenditures for Property, Plant, and Equipment	$(3,050)	
Expenditures for Intangible Assets	(575)	(3,625)
Cash Flow from Financing Activities		
Increase in Short-Term Debt	$ 125	
Increase in Long-Term Debt	500	
Issuance of Additional Capital Stock Shares	175	
Distribution of Cash Dividends from Profit	(750)	50
Decrease in Cash During Year		$ (470)
Cash Balance at Start of Year		3,735
Cash Balance at End of Year		$ 3,265

Income Statement

The first question on everyone's mind usually is whether a business made a profit, and, if so, how much. So, we'll start with the income statement and then move on to the balance sheet and statement of cash flows. The income statement summarizes sales revenue and expenses for a period of time—one year in Exhibit 2.2. All the dollar amounts reported in this financial statement are cumulative totals for the whole period.

The top line is the total amount of proceeds or gross income from sales to customers, and is generally called *sales revenue*. The bottom line is called *net income* (also net earnings, but hardly ever profit or net profit). Net income is the final profit after all expenses are deducted from sales revenue. The business in this example earned $2,642,000 net income on its sales revenue of $52,000,000 for the year; only 5.1% of its sales revenue remained as final profit (net income) after deducting all expenses.

The income statement is designed to be read in a step-down manner, like walking down stairs. Each step down is a deduction of one or more expenses. The first step deducts the cost of goods (products) sold from the sales revenue of goods sold, which gives *gross margin* (sometimes called gross profit—one of the few instances of using the term profit in income statements). This measure of profit is called "gross" because many other expenses are not yet deducted.

Next, the broad category of operating expenses called selling, general, and administrative expenses and the depreciation expense (a unique expense) are deducted from gross margin, giving *earnings before interest and income tax*. This measure of profit is also called *operating earnings*, or a similar title. Next, interest expense on debt is deducted, which gives earnings before income tax. The last step is to deduct income tax expense, which gives net income, the bottom line in the income statement.

Instead of the multiple-step income statement shown in Exhibit 2.2, which has three intermediate measures of profit, you may see a single-step income statement that reports only the final line of net income, which is shown in Exhibit 2.4.

Publicly owned business corporations are required to report *earnings per share* (EPS), which is net income divided by the number of stock shares. Privately owned businesses don't have to report EPS, but this figure may be useful to their stockholders. I explain earnings per share in Chapters 12 and 17.

EXHIBIT 2.4—SINGLE-STEP INCOME STATEMENT
Dollar Amounts in Thousands

Sales Revenue	$ 52,000
Cost of Goods Sold Expense	(33,800)
Selling, General, and Administrative Expenses	(12,480)
Depreciation Expense	(785)
Interest Expense	(545)
Income Tax Expense	(1,748)
Net Income	$ 2,642

In our income statement example you see five different expenses. You may find more expense lines in an income statement, but seldom more than 10 or so as a general rule (unless the business had a very unusual year). Companies selling products are required to report their cost of goods sold expense. Some companies do not report depreciation expense on a separate line in their income statements. However, depreciation is such a unique expense that I prefer to keep it separate from the other expenses.

Other than depreciation, Exhibit 2.2 includes just one broad, all-inclusive operating expenses line—"Selling, General, and Administrative Expenses." However, a business may report two or more operating expenses. Marketing, promotional, and selling expenses often are separated from general and administration expenses. The level of detail for expenses in income statements is flexible; financial reporting standards are somewhat loose on this point.

The sales revenue and expenses reported in income statements follow generally accepted conventions, which are briefly summarized here:

- **Sales Revenue**—the total amount received or to be received from the sales of products (and/or services) to customers during the period. Sales revenue is *net*, which means that discounts off list prices, prompt payment discounts, sales returns, and any other deductions from original sales prices are deducted to determine the sales revenue amount for the period. Sales taxes are not included in sales revenue, nor are excise taxes that might apply. In short, sales revenue is the amount the business should receive to cover its expenses and to provide profit (bottom-line net income).

- **Cost of Goods Sold Expense**—the total cost of goods (products) sold to customers during the period. This is clear enough. What might not be so clear, however, concerns goods that were shoplifted or are otherwise missing, as well as write-downs due to damage and obsolescence. The cost of such *inventory shrinkage* may be included in cost of goods sold expense for the year (or, this cost may be put in another expense account instead).

- **Selling, General, and Administrative Expenses (Operating Expenses)**—broadly speaking, every expense other than cost of goods sold, depreciation, interest, and income tax. This broad category is a catchall for every expense not reported separately. In our example, depreciation is broken out as separate expense instead of being included with other operating expenses. Some companies report advertising and marketing costs separately from administrative and general costs, and some report research and development expenses separately. There are hundreds of specific operating expenses, some rather large and some very small. They range from salaries and wages of employees (large) to legal fees (small, one hopes).

- **Depreciation Expense**—the portion of original costs of long-term assets such as buildings, machinery, equipment, tools, furniture, computers, and vehicles that is recorded to expense in one period. Depreciation is the "charge" for using these assets during the period. None of this expense amount is a cash outlay in the period recorded, which makes it a unique expense compared with other operating expenses.

- **Interest Expense**—the amount of interest on debt (interest-bearing liabilities) for the period. Other types of financing charges may also be included, such as loan origination fees.

- **Income Tax Expense**—the total amount due the government (both federal and state) on the amount of taxable income of the business during the period. Taxable income is multiplied by the appropriate tax rates. The income tax expense does not include other types of taxes, such as unemployment and Social Security taxes on the company's payroll. These other, non-income taxes are included in operating expenses.

Balance Sheet

The balance sheet shown in Exhibit 2.1 follows the standardized format regarding the classification and ordering of assets, liabilities, and ownership interests in the business. Financial institutions, public utilities, railroads, and some other specialized businesses use different balance sheet layouts. However, manufacturers and retailers, as well as the large majority of other types of businesses, follow the format presented in Exhibit 2.1.

On the left side the balance sheet lists *assets*. On the right side the balance sheet first lists the *liabilities* of the business, which have a higher-order claim on the assets. The sources of ownership (equity) capital in the business are presented below the liabilities, to emphasize that the owners or equity holders in a business (the stockholders of a business corporation) have a secondary and lower order claim on the assets—after its liabilities are satisfied.

Each separate asset, liability, and stockholders' equity reported in a balance sheet is called an *account*. Every account has a name (title) and a dollar amount, which is called its *balance*. For instance, from Exhibit 2.1 at the end of the most recent year:

Name of Account	Amount (Balance) of Account
Inventory	$8,450,000

The other dollar amounts in the balance sheet are either sub-totals or totals of account balances. For example, the $17,675,000 amount for "Current Assets" does not represent an account but rather the subtotal of the four accounts making up this group of accounts. A line is drawn above a subtotal or total, indicating account balances are being added.

A double underline (such as for "Total Assets") indicates the last amount in a column. Notice also the double underline below "Net Income" in the income statement (Exhibit 2.2), indicating it is the last number in the column.

A balance sheet is prepared at the close of business on the last day of the income statement period. For example, if the income statement is for the year ending June 30, 2009, the balance sheet is prepared at midnight June 30, 2009. The amounts reported in the balance sheet are the balances of the accounts at that precise moment in time. The financial condition of the business is frozen for one split second.

The balance sheet does not report the flows of activities in the company's assets, liabilities, and shareowners' equity accounts during the period. Only the ending balances at the moment the balance sheet is prepared are reported for the accounts. For example, the company reports an ending cash balance of $3,265,000 at the end of its most recent year (see Exhibit 2.1). Can you tell the total cash inflows and outflows for the year? No, not from the balance sheet; you can't even get a clue from the balance sheet alone.

The accounts reported in the balance sheet are not thrown together haphazardly in no particular order. According to long-standing rules, balance sheet accounts are subdivided into the following classes, or basic groups, in the following order of presentation:

Left (or Top) Side	*Right (or Bottom) Side*
Current assets	Current liabilities
Long-term operating assets	Long-term liabilities
Other assets	Owners' equity

Current assets are cash and other assets that will be converted into cash during one *operating cycle*. The operating cycle refers to the sequence of buying or manufacturing products, holding the products until sale, selling the products, waiting to collect the receivables from the sales, and finally receiving cash from customers. This sequence is the most basic rhythm of a company's operations; it is repeated over and over. The operating cycle may be short, only 60 days or less, or it may be relatively long, taking 180 days or more.

Assets not directly required in the operating cycle, such as marketable securities held as temporary investments or short-term loans made to employees, are included in the current assets class if they will be converted into cash during the coming year. A business pays in advance for some costs of operations that will not be charged to expense until next period. These *prepaid expenses* are included in current assets, as you see in Exhibit 2.1.

The second group of assets is labeled "Long-Term Operating Assets" in the balance sheet. These assets are not held for sale to customers; rather, they are used in the operations of the business. Broadly speaking, these assets fall into two groups: *tangible* and *intangible* assets. Tangible assets have physical existence, such as machines and buildings. Intangible assets do not have physical existence, but they are legally protected rights (such as patents and trademarks), or they are such things as secret processes and well-known favorable reputations that give businesses important competitive advantages.

The tangible assets of the business are reported in the "Property, Plant, and Equipment" account—see Exhibit 2.1 again. More informally, these assets are called *fixed assets*, although this term is generally not used in balance sheets. The word *fixed* is a little strong; these assets are not really fixed or permanent, except for the land owned by a business. More accurately, these assets are the long-term operating resources used over several years—such as buildings, machinery, equipment, trucks, forklifts, furniture, computers, telephones, and so on.

The cost of a fixed asset—with the exception of land—is gradually charged off over its useful life. Each period of use thereby bears its share of the total cost of each fixed asset. This apportionment of the cost of fixed assets over their useful lives is called *depreciation*. The amount of depreciation for one year is reported as an expense in the income statement (see Exhibit 2.2). The cumulative amount that has been recorded as depreciation expense since the date of acquisition up to the balance sheet date is reported in the *accumulated depreciation* account in the balance sheet (see Exhibit 2.1). As you see, the balance in the accumulated depreciation account is deducted from the original cost of the fixed assets.

In the example, the business owns various intangible long-term operating assets. These assets are recorded at the cost of acquisition. The cost of an intangible asset remains on the books until the business determines that the asset has lost value or no longer has economic benefit. At that time the business writes down (or writes off) the original cost of the intangible asset and charges the amount to an expense, usually *amortization expense*. Until recently, the general practice was to allocate the cost of intangible assets over arbitrary time periods. However, many intangible assets have indefinite and indeterminable useful lives. The conventional wisdom now is that it's better to wait until an intangible asset has lost value, at which time an expense is recorded.

Other assets is a catchall title for those assets that don't fit in the current assets or long-term operating assets classes. The company in this example does not have any such "other" assets.

The accounts reported in the *current liabilities* class are short-term liabilities that for the most part depend on the conversion of current assets into cash for their payment. Also, other debts (borrowed money) that will come due within one year from the balance sheet date are put in this group. In our example, there are four accounts in current liabilities (see Exhibit 2.1 again).

Long-term liabilities (labeled "Long-Term Notes Payable" in Exhibit 2.1) are those whose maturity dates are more than one year after the balance sheet date. There's only one such account in our example. Either in the balance sheet or in a footnote, the maturity dates, interest rates, and other relevant provisions of long-term liabilities are disclosed. To simplify, no footnotes are included with our financial statements example (Chapter 15 discusses footnotes).

Liabilities are claims on the assets of a business; cash or other assets that will be later converted into cash will be used to pay the liabilities. (Also, cash generated by future profit earned by the business will be available to pay its liabilities.) Clearly, all liabilities of a business must be reported in its balance sheet to give a complete picture of the financial condition of a business.

Liabilities are also sources of assets. For example, cash increases when a business borrows money. Inventory increases when a business buys products on credit and incurs a liability that will be paid later. Also, typically a business has liabilities for unpaid expenses and has not yet used cash to pay these liabilities.

Another reason for reporting liabilities in the balance sheet is to account for the sources of the company's assets—to answer the question: Where did the company's total assets come from? A complete picture of the financial condition of a business shows where the company's assets came from.

Some part of the total assets of a business comes not from liabilities but from its owners. The owners invest money in the business and the business retains some of its profit, which is not distributed to its owners. In this example the business is organized as a corporation. Its *stockholders' equity* accounts in the balance sheet reveal where the excess of the company's total assets over its total liabilities came from. Notice in Exhibit 2.1 that there are two stockholders' (owners') equity sources—*capital stock* and *retained earnings*.

When owners (stockholders of a business corporation) invest capital in the business, the capital stock account is increased.* Net income earned by a business less the amount distributed to owners increases the retained earnings account. The nature of retained earnings can be confusing; therefore, I explain this account in depth at the appropriate places in the book. Just a quick word of advice here: Retained earnings is *not*—I repeat, is *not*—an asset. Get such a notion out of your head.

---

*Many business corporations issue *par value* stock shares. The shares have to be issued for a certain minimum amount, called the par value, but the corporation may issue the shares for more than par value. The excess over par value is put in a second account called "Paid-In Capital in Excess of Par Value." This is not shown in the balance sheet example, because the separation between the two accounts has little practical significance for financial reporting.

Statement of Cash Flows

Exhibit 2.3 presents the company's statement of cash flows for the same year as its income statement (Exhibit 2.2). The balance sheets at the start and end of the year can be thought of as the bookends of the company's two activity statements—the income statement and the cash flows statement. The two activity statements reveal the reasons for the changes in the company's financial condition from the start of the year to the end of the year.

I explain the statement of cash flows extensively in Chapters 13 and 14. At this point I simply introduce this financial statement.

If you compare the informal summary of cash flows presented in Chapter 1 (Exhibit 1.1) with the formal statement of cash flows in this chapter (Exhibit 2.3), you see several differences.

You might think that the financial statement that summarizes cash flows would be fairly simple and straightforward. But I regret to tell you that the statement of cash flows is more involved than meets the eye. To understand cash flows, you must first have a good grasp of the income statement and balance sheet and how those two financial statements are connected.

3

PROFIT ISN'T EVERYTHING

The Threefold Task of Business Managers:
Profit, Financial Condition, and Cash Flows

The income statement reports the profit performance of a business. The ability of managers to make sales and to control expenses, and thereby earn profit, is summarized in the income statement. Earning adequate profit is the key for survival and the business manager's most important financial imperative. But the bottom line is not the end of the manager's job, not by a long shot!

To earn profit and stay out of trouble, managers must control the *financial condition* of the business. This means, among other things, keeping assets and liabilities within proper limits and proportions relative to each other and relative to the sales revenue and expenses of the business. Managers must, in particular, prevent cash shortages that would cause the business to default on its liabilities when they come due, or not be able to meet its payroll on time.

Business managers really have a threefold task: earning enough profit, controlling the company's assets and liabilities, and controlling cash flows. Earning profit by itself does not guarantee survival and good cash flow. A business manager cannot manage profit without also managing the changes in financial condition caused by sales and expenses that produce profit. Making profit may actually cause a temporary drain on cash rather than provide cash.

A business manager should use his or her income statement to evaluate profit performance and to ask a raft of profit-oriented questions. Did sales revenue meet the goals and objectives for the period? Why did sales revenue increase compared with last period? Which expenses increased more or less than they should have? And there are many more such questions. These profit analysis questions are absolutely essential. But the manager can't stop at the end of these questions.

Beyond profit analysis, business managers should move on to financial condition analysis and cash flows analysis. In large business corporations, the responsibility for financial condition and cash flows typically is separated from profit responsibility. The chief financial officer (CFO) of the company is responsible for financial condition and cash flows. The chief executive and board of directors oversee the CFO. They need to see the big picture, which includes all three financial aspects of the business—profit, financial condition, and cash flow.

In smaller businesses, however, the president or the owner/manager is directly and totally involved in controlling financial condition and cash flow. There's no one to whom to delegate these responsibilities.

For all businesses, regardless of size, a financial statement is prepared for each financial imperative—one for profit performance (the income statement), one for financial condition (the balance sheet), and the statement of cash flows.

One Problem in Reporting Financial Statements

Unfortunately, the way financial statements are presented to business managers and other interested readers does not pave the way for understanding how making profit drives the financial condition and cash flows of the business. You can miss the vital interplay among the income statement, balance sheet, and cash flows because each statement is presented like a tub standing on its own feet. The "water pipes" (interconnections) between the three financial statements are not made explicit.

Exhibits 2.1, 2.2, and 2.3 in Chapter 2 present the balance sheet, income statement, and statement of cash flows for a business, as you would see these three primary financial statements. Each of the statements stands alone, by itself as an island. This is the standard way of presenting financial statements in a financial report. There is no clear trail of the crossover effects between the basic financial statements. The statements are presented on the assumption that readers understand the couplings and linkages between the financial statements and that readers make appropriate comparisons.

In contrast, see Exhibit 3.1, which shows the lines of connection between the income statement and the balance sheet, and the lines of connection between the changes in the balance sheet accounts and the statement of cash flows.

The main message of this chapter is that the three basic financial statements fit together like tongue-in-groove woodwork. The income statement, balance sheet, and cash flows statement interlock with one another, which the following discussion explains.

EXHIBIT 3.1—CONNECTIONS BETWEEN THREE FINANCIAL STATEMENTS

Dollar Amounts in Thousands

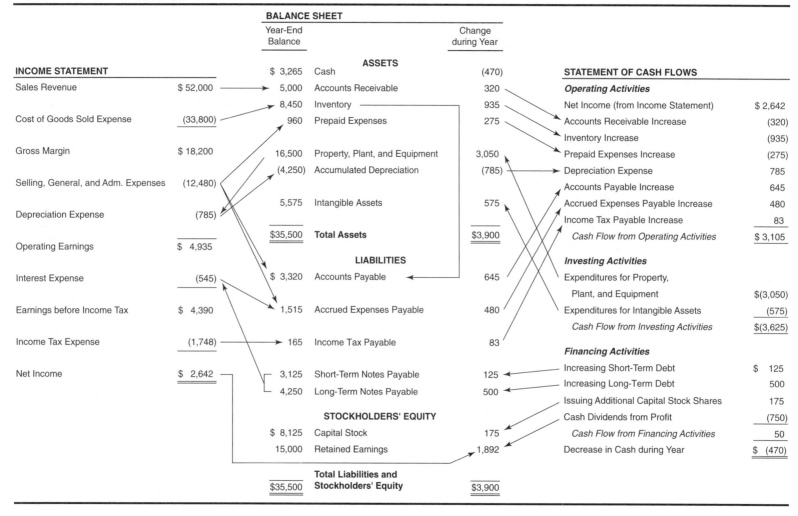

INCOME STATEMENT		BALANCE SHEET			STATEMENT OF CASH FLOWS	
		Year-End Balance		Change during Year		
			ASSETS			
		$ 3,265	Cash	(470)		
Sales Revenue	$ 52,000	5,000	Accounts Receivable	320	**Operating Activities**	
		8,450	Inventory	935	Net Income (from Income Statement)	$ 2,642
Cost of Goods Sold Expense	(33,800)	960	Prepaid Expenses	275	Accounts Receivable Increase	(320)
					Inventory Increase	(935)
Gross Margin	$ 18,200	16,500	Property, Plant, and Equipment	3,050	Prepaid Expenses Increase	(275)
		(4,250)	Accumulated Depreciation	(785)	Depreciation Expense	785
Selling, General, and Adm. Expenses	(12,480)				Accounts Payable Increase	645
		5,575	Intangible Assets	575	Accrued Expenses Payable Increase	480
Depreciation Expense	(785)				Income Tax Payable Increase	83
		$35,500	**Total Assets**	$3,900	Cash Flow from Operating Activities	$ 3,105
Operating Earnings	$ 4,935		**LIABILITIES**			
Interest Expense	(545)	$ 3,320	Accounts Payable	645	**Investing Activities**	
					Expenditures for Property,	
					Plant, and Equipment	$(3,050)
Earnings before Income Tax	$ 4,390	1,515	Accrued Expenses Payable	480	Expenditures for Intangible Assets	(575)
					Cash Flow from Investing Activities	$(3,625)
Income Tax Expense	(1,748)	165	Income Tax Payable	83		
					Financing Activities	
Net Income	$ 2,642	3,125	Short-Term Notes Payable	125	Increasing Short-Term Debt	$ 125
		4,250	Long-Term Notes Payable	500	Increasing Long-Term Debt	500
					Issuing Additional Capital Stock Shares	175
			STOCKHOLDERS' EQUITY		Cash Dividends from Profit	(750)
		$ 8,125	Capital Stock	175	Cash Flow from Financing Activities	50
		15,000	Retained Earnings	1,892	Decrease in Cash during Year	$ (470)
		$35,500	**Total Liabilities and Stockholders' Equity**	$3,900		

The Interlocking Nature of the Three Financial Statements

Exhibit 3.1 demonstrates how the financial statements of a business are interconnected. First, it shows the lines of connection between the income statement and the balance sheet. Notice in passing that the balance sheet is presented in a *vertical* format, called the "report form"—assets on top, and liabilities and stockholders' equity below. In fact, many balance sheets are presented in the report form.

Sales revenue drives the *accounts receivable* asset account—see the first line of connection in Exhibit 3.1. Cost of goods sold expense drives the *inventory* asset account—see the second line of connection in the exhibit. And so on. We'll move carefully through each of these connections one at a time in the following chapters. Chapter 4 explores the linkage between sales revenue in the income statement and accounts receivable in the balance sheet. Then each connection is explored in successive chapters.

Exhibit 3.1 presents the balance sheet of the business at the end of the company's most recent year—at midnight on the last day of the year for which the income statement is prepared—and also shows the changes in each account during the year, which tie in with the statement of cash flows. Virtually all the company's assets, liabilities, and owners' equity sources had different balances at the start of the year. Certain of these changes have the effect of increasing or decreasing the amount of cash flow from the company's profit-making activities for the year.

In other words, the net cash increase (or decrease, as the case may be) during the year from its revenue and expenses depends on the changes in certain of the company's assets and liabilities. Exhibit 3.1 shows these connections. Notice that the lines of connection go from the changes in the balance sheet to increases or decreases in net income, in order to put net income on the cash flows basis—or, to be more accurate, I should say to determine the cash flows result from the company's sales revenue and expenses for the year.

The end result is that the cash increase from the company's profit-making activities for the year is $3,105,000, which compared with its $2,642,000 net income is a fairly significant difference. In the example, for the year the company's cash flow from profit is $463,000 higher than its profit for the year. In other situations, cash flow from profit could be much less than net income.

During the year the business had other cash flows that changed certain assets, liabilities, and owners' equity items. These are also shown in Exhibit 3.1. Notice that the lines of connection go from the cash flow sources and uses to their corresponding balance sheet accounts. The cash flow sources and uses drive the changes in the balance sheet.

You really can't swallow all the information in Exhibit 3.1 in one gulp. You have to drink one sip at a time. Exhibit 3.1 serves as the road map that we'll refer to frequently in the following chapters—so that we don't lose sight of the big picture as we travel down the particular highways of connection between the financial statements.

Before moving on, let me stress that financial statements are not presented with lines of connection as shown in Exhibit 3.1. You never see such tether lines between the components of the financial statements. Accountants assume that the financial statement readers mentally fill in the connections that are shown in Exhibit 3.1. Accountants assume too much, in my opinion. It would be helpful if financial reports included reminders of the connections among the three financial statements. But don't hold your breath.

Connecting the Dots

In my experience, business managers and executives, and for that matter even some certified public accountants (CPAs), do not recognize the connecting links among the financial statements that I show in Exhibit 3.1. Over the years I have corresponded with many persons who have contacted me requesting the Excel workbook file of the exhibits in this book. (See the Preface for my e-mail address.) Over and over they mention one point—the value of seeing the connections among the financial statements.

I did not fully understand these connections myself until I started teaching at the University of California at Berkeley in 1961. In browsing through an old, out-of-print textbook, I came upon the point that financial statements, although presented separately, are articulated with one another. Even though I had already earned my Ph.D., I had not seen this critical point before. (Or perhaps I had slept through that particular lecture in college.) I was struck by the term "articulated." In my mind's eye I could see an articulated bus, a bus having two compartments that were connected together.

Exhibit 3.1 provides the framework for the following several chapters. Each chapter focuses on one key connection between the financial statements. I hope you find the financial trip in the following chapters interesting and useful. I think you will.

EXHIBIT 4.1—SALES REVENUE AND ACCOUNTS RECEIVABLE

Dollar Amounts in Thousands

BALANCE SHEET AT YEAR-END

ASSETS

Cash	$ 3,265
Accounts Receivable	5,000
Inventory	8,450
Prepaid Expenses	960
Property, Plant, and Equipment	16,500
Accumulated Depreciation	(4,250)
Intangible Assets	5,575
Total Assets	$35,500

Assuming five weeks of annual sales revenue is uncollected at year-end, the ending balance of Accounts Receivable is:

$5/52 \times \$52,000 = \$5,000$

INCOME STATEMENT FOR YEAR

Sales Revenue	$ 52,000
Cost of Goods Sold Expense	(33,800)
Selling, General, and Adm. Expenses	(12,480)
Depreciation Expense	(785)
Interest Expense	(545)
Income Tax Expense	(1,748)
Net Income	$ 2,642

LIABILITIES and STOCKHOLDERS' EQUITY

Accounts Payable	$ 3,320
Accrued Expenses Payable	1,515
Income Tax Payable	165
Short-Term Notes Payable	3,125
Long-Term Notes Payable	4,250
Capital Stock	8,125
Retained Earnings	15,000
Total Liabilities and Stockholders' Equity	$35,500

4

SALES REVENUE AND ACCOUNTS RECEIVABLE

Exploring One Link at a Time

Please refer to Exhibit 4.1 at the start of the chapter, which shows the connection between *sales revenue* in the income statement and the *accounts receivable* asset account in the balance sheet. This exhibit is taken from Exhibit 3.1 in Chapter 3. Exhibit 3.1 presents the big picture; it ties together all the connections between the income statement and the balance sheet. This chapter is the first of many that focus on just one connection at a time. Only one line of connection is highlighted in Exhibit 4.1—the one between sales revenue in the income statement and accounts receivable in the balance sheet.

Friendly Reminder: In Exhibit 4.1 (and all those exhibits to follow in the coming chapters) the income statement and balance sheet are stripped of subtotals. For example, the income statement is a single-step statement, meaning that no lines are shown for gross margin and other intermediate measures of profit. Likewise, in the balance sheet no subtotals are shown for current assets and current liabilities and for the amount of property, plant, and equipment less accumulated depreciation.

Excluding subtotals gives us lean and mean financial statements to work with.

Another Friendly Reminder: Exhibit 4.1 does not include the company's statement of cash flows for the year. The connections between changes in the balance sheet accounts and the cash flows statement are explained in Chapters 13 and 14. The cash flows statement would be a distraction at this point.

The central idea in this and following chapters is that the profit-making activities reported in the income statement drive, or determine, an asset or a liability. Assets and liabilities are reported in the balance sheet. For example, the company's sales revenue for the year just ended was $52 million. Of this total sales revenue, $5 million is in the accounts receivable asset account at the end of the year. The $5 million is that part of annual sales that had not yet been collected at the end of the year.

In the following chapters we explore each linkage between an income statement account and its connecting account in the balance sheet.

How Sales Revenue Drives Accounts Receivable

In this business example, the company made $52,000,000 total sales during the year. This is a sizable amount, equal to $1,000,000 average sales revenue per week. When making a sale, the total amount of the sale (sales price times the quantity of products sold) is recorded in the *sales revenue* account. This account accumulates all sales made during the year. On the first day of the year it starts with a zero balance; at the end of the last day of the year it has a $52,000,000 balance. In short, the balance in this account at year-end is the sum of all sales for the entire year (assuming all sales are recorded, of course).

In this example, the business makes all its sales on credit, which means that cash is not received until sometime after the time of sale. This company sells to other businesses that demand credit. (Many retailers, such as supermarkets and gas stations, make all sales for cash, or accept credit cards that are converted into cash immediately.) The amount owed to the company from making a sale on credit is immediately recorded in the accounts receivable asset account for the amount of each sale. Sometime later, when cash is collected from customers, the cash account is increased and the accounts receivable account is decreased.

Extending credit to customers creates a cash inflow lag. The accounts receivable balance is the amount of this lag. At year-end the balance in this asset account is the amount of uncollected sales revenue. Most of the sales made on credit during the year have been converted into cash by the end of the year. Also, the accounts receivable balance at the start of the year from

credit sales made last year was collected. But, many sales made during the latter part of the year have not yet been collected by year-end. The total amount of these uncollected sales is found in the ending balance of accounts receivable.

Some of the company's customers pay quickly to take advantage of prompt payment discounts offered by the company. (These discounts off list prices reduce sales prices but speed up cash receipts.) However, the average customer waits five weeks to pay the company and forgoes the prompt payment discount. Some customers even wait 10 weeks or more to pay the company, despite the company's efforts to encourage them to pay sooner. The company puts up with these slow payers because they generate a lot of repeat sales.

In sum, the company has a mix of quick, regular, and slow-paying customers. Suppose that the average credit period for all customers is five weeks. (This doesn't mean every customer takes five weeks to pay, but rather that the average time before paying is five weeks.) This means that on average five weeks of annual sales were still uncollected at year-end. The relationship between annual sales revenue and the ending balance of accounts receivable, therefore, can be expressed as follows:

$$\frac{5}{52} \times \frac{\$52,000,000 \text{ Sales}}{\text{Revenue for the Year}} = \frac{\$5,000,000 \text{ Accounts}}{\text{Receivable at End of Year}}$$

As you see in Exhibit 4.1, the ending balance of accounts receivable is $5,000,000; this equals five weeks of annual sales revenue. The main point is that the average sales credit period determines the size of accounts receivable. The longer the average sales credit period, the larger the accounts receivable amount.

Let's approach this key point from another direction. Suppose we didn't know the average credit period. Nevertheless, using information from the financial statements we can determine the average credit period. The first step is to calculate the following ratio:

$$\frac{\$52,000,000 \text{ Sales Revenue}}{\$5,000,000 \text{ Accounts Receivable}} = 10.4 \text{ Times}$$

This calculation gives the *accounts receivable turnover ratio*, which is 10.4 in this example. Dividing this ratio into 52 weeks gives the average sales credit period expressed in number of weeks:

$$\frac{52 \text{ Weeks}}{10.4 \text{ Accounts Receivable Turnover Ratio}} = 5 \text{ Weeks}$$

Time is the essence of the matter. What interests the business manager, and the company's creditors and investors as well, is how long it takes on average to turn accounts receivable into cash. I think the accounts receivable turnover ratio is most meaningful when it is used to determine the number of weeks (or days, if you like) it takes a company to convert its accounts receivable into cash.

You may argue that five weeks is too long an average sales credit period for the company. This is precisely the point: What should it be? The manager in charge has to decide whether the average credit period is getting out of hand. The manager can shorten credit terms, shut off credit to slow payers, or step up collection efforts.

This isn't the place to discuss customer credit policies relative to marketing strategies and customer relations, which would take us far beyond the field of accounting. But, to make an important point here, assume that without losing any sales the company's average sales credit period had been only four weeks, instead of five weeks.

In this alternative scenario, the company's ending accounts receivable balance would have been $1,000,000 less, or $4,000,000 (4/52 × $52,000,000 annual sales revenue = $4,000,000). The company would have collected $1,000,000 more cash during the year. With this additional cash, the company could have borrowed $1,000,000 less. At an annual 6% interest rate, this would have saved the business $60,000 interest before income tax. Or the owners could have invested $1,000,000 less in the business and put their money elsewhere.

The main point, of course, is that capital has a cost. Excess accounts receivable means that excess debt or excess owners' equity capital is being used by the business. The business is not as capital efficient as it should be.

A slowdown in collecting customers' receivables or a deliberate shift in business policy allowing longer credit terms causes accounts receivable to increase. Additional capital would have to be secured, or the company would have to attempt to get by on a smaller cash balance.

If you were the business manager in this example, you should decide whether the size of accounts receivable, being five weeks of annual sales revenue, is consistent with your company's sales credit terms and your collection policies. Perhaps five weeks is too long and you need to take action. If you were a creditor or an investor in the company, you should pay attention to whether the manager is allowing the average sales credit period to get out of control. A major change in the average credit period may signal a significant change in the company's policies.

Accounting Issues

Starting in this chapter and continuing in the following chapters that focus on the key connections between an income statement account and its corresponding balance sheet account, I end the chapter with a very brief discussion of the major accounting problems pertaining to the accounts discussed in the chapter.

These short discussions of accounting issues barely scratch the surface. Nevertheless, you should be aware that the numbers you see in financial statements depend on the accounting methods used to generate those numbers. The chief accounting officer of every business has to decide which accounting methods to use to record sales revenue and expenses.

You may not be aware that these accounting decisions are not entirely obvious and clear-cut in most situations. As a matter of fact, accounting methods are arbitrary to one degree or another in most cases. The choice of particular accounting methods makes profit lower or higher and also makes the amounts of assets and liabilities lower or higher.

So, what are the main issues in accounting for sales and accounts receivable? The main problem in recording sales is *timing*. It's not always clear exactly when a sale is completed and all terms are final. Customers may have the right to return products they have purchased. Customers may have the right to take discounts from sales prices after the point of sale. Sales prices may still be negotiable even after the point of sale. Then, there are the costs of product warranties and guarantees to consider.

The asset generated by credit sales (i.e., accounts receivable) may end up being not collectible, or not fully collectible. When should the business record the expense for uncollectible receivables (called *bad debts*)?

In short, there are several serious problems surrounding accounting for sales. Therefore, a business should make clear in the footnotes to its financial statements the basic accounting method it uses for recording sales revenue.

EXHIBIT 5.1—COST OF GOODS SOLD EXPENSE AND INVENTORY

Dollar Amounts in Thousands

INCOME STATEMENT FOR YEAR

Sales Revenue	$ 52,000
Cost of Goods Sold Expense	(33,800)
Selling, General, and Adm. Expenses	(12,480)
Depreciation Expense	(785)
Interest Expense	(545)
Income Tax Expense	(1,748)
Net Income	$ 2,642

Assuming the year-end inventory of goods awaiting sale equals 13 weeks of annual cost of goods sold, the ending balance of Inventory is:

$$13/52 \times \$33,800 = \$8,450$$

BALANCE SHEET AT YEAR-END

ASSETS

Cash	$ 3,265
Accounts Receivable	5,000
Inventory	8,450
Prepaid Expenses	960
Property, Plant, and Equipment	16,500
Accumulated Depreciation	(4,250)
Intangible Assets	5,575
Total Assets	$35,500

LIABILITIES and STOCKHOLDERS' EQUITY

Accounts Payable	$ 3,320
Accrued Expenses Payable	1,515
Income Tax Payable	165
Short-Term Notes Payable	3,125
Long-Term Notes Payable	4,250
Capital Stock	8,125
Retained Earnings	15,000
Total Liabilities and Stockholders' Equity	$35,500

5

COST OF GOODS SOLD EXPENSE AND INVENTORY

Holding Products in Inventory Before They Are Sold

Please refer to Exhibit 5.1 at the start of the chapter. (Chapter 4 explains the design of this exhibit, which is also used in following chapters.) This chapter focuses on the connection between *cost of goods sold expense* in the income statement and the *inventory* asset in the balance sheet. Recall that the business in the example sells products, which are also called "goods" or "merchandise."

Cost of goods sold expense means just that—the cost of all products sold to customers during the year. The revenue from the sales is recorded in the sales revenue account, which is reported just above the cost of goods sold expense in the income statement (see Exhibit 5.1). Cost of goods sold expense is by far the largest expense in the company's income statement, being almost three times its selling, general, and administrative expenses for the year.

Putting cost of goods sold expense first, at the head of the expenses, is logical because it's the most direct and immediate cost of selling products. Please recall that this expense is deducted from sales revenue in income statements so that *gross margin* is reported there—see Exhibit 2.2 for an example of an income statement. Although gross margin is not shown on a separate line in Exhibit 5.1, in order to focus on the key connections of income statement and balance sheet accounts, I can't emphasize enough the importance of gross margin (also called gross profit).

The word "gross" emphasizes that no other expenses have been deducted from sales revenue yet. Of course, there are more expenses that must be deducted before arriving at bottom-line profit (net income). Gross margin is the starting point for earning an adequate final, bottom-line profit for the period. In other words, the first step is to sell products for enough gross margin so that all other expenses can be covered and still leave an adequate remainder of profit. Later chapters discuss the company's other expenses.

You can do the arithmetic and determine that cost of goods sold expense equals 65% of sales revenue. Therefore, gross margin equals 35% of sales revenue. The business sells many different products, some for more than 35% gross margin and some for less. In total, for all products sold during the year, its average gross margin is 35%—which is fairly typical for a broad cross section of businesses. Gross margins more than 50% or less than 20% are unusual.

To sell products, most businesses must keep a stock of products on hand, which is called *inventory*. If a company sells products, it would be a real shock to see no inventory in its balance sheet (it is possible, but highly unlikely). Notice in Exhibit 5.1 that the line of connection is not between sales revenue and inventory, but between cost of goods sold expense and inventory. The inventory asset is reported at cost in the balance sheet, not at its sales value.

The inventory asset account accumulates the cost of the products purchased or manufactured. Acquisition cost stays in an inventory asset account until the products are sold to customers. At this time, the cost of the products is removed from inventory and charged out to cost of goods sold expense. (Products may become nonsalable or may be stolen or damaged, in which case their cost is written down or removed from inventory and the amount is charged to cost of goods sold or some other expense, which I discuss at the end of the chapter.)

The company's inventory balance at year-end—$8,450,000 in this example—is the cost of products awaiting sale next year. The $33,800,000 deducted from sales revenue in the income statement is the cost of goods that were sold during the year. Of course none of these products were on hand in year-end inventory.

Some of the company's products are manufactured in a short time, and some take much longer. Once the production process is finished, the products are moved into the company warehouse for storage until the goods are sold and delivered to customers. Some products are sold quickly, almost right off the end of the production line. Other products sit in the warehouse many weeks before being sold. This business, like most companies, sells a mix of different products—some of which have very short holding periods and some very long holding periods.

In this example, the company's *average* inventory holding period for all products is 13 weeks, or three months on average. This time interval includes the production process time and the warehouse storage time. For example, a product may take three weeks to manufacture and then be held in storage 10 weeks, or vice versa. Internally, manufacturers separate "work-in-process" inventory (products still in the process of being manufactured) from "finished goods" (completed inventory ready for delivery to customers). Usually only one combined inventory account is reported in the external balance sheet, as shown in Exhibit 5.1.

Given that its average inventory holding period is 13 weeks, the company's inventory cost can be expressed as follows:

$$\frac{13}{52} \times \begin{array}{c} \$33,800,000 \\ \text{Cost of Goods Sold} \\ \text{Expense for Year} \end{array} = \begin{array}{c} \$8,450,000 \\ \text{Inventory} \\ \text{at End of Year} \end{array}$$

Notice in Exhibit 5.1 that the company's ending inventory balance is $8,450,000.

The main point is that the average inventory holding period determines the size of inventory relative to annual cost of goods sold. The longer the manufacturing and warehouse holding period, the larger is the inventory amount. Business managers prefer to operate with the lowest level of inventory possible, without causing lost sales due to products being out of stock when customers want to buy them. A business invests substantial capital in inventory.

Now, suppose we didn't know the company's average inventory holding period. Using information from its financial statements, we can determine the average inventory holding period.

The first step is to calculate the following ratio:

$$\frac{\$33,800,000 \text{ Cost of Goods Sold Expense}}{\$8,450,000 \text{ Inventory}} = 4.00 \text{ Times}$$

This gives the *inventory turnover ratio*. Dividing this ratio into 52 weeks gives the average inventory holding period expressed in number of weeks:

$$\frac{52 \text{ Weeks}}{4.00 \text{ Inventory Turnover Ratio}} = 13 \text{ Weeks}$$

Time is the essence of the matter, as with the average sales credit period extended to customers. What interests the managers, as well as the company's creditors and investors, is how long the company holds inventory before products are sold. I think the inventory turnover ratio is most meaningful when used to determine the number of weeks (or days if you prefer) that it takes before inventory is sold.

Is 13 weeks too long? Should the company's average inventory holding period be shorter? These are precisely the key questions business managers, creditors, and investors should obtain answers to. If the holding period is longer than necessary, too much capital is being tied up in inventory. Or, the company may be cash poor because it keeps too much money in inventory and not enough in the bank.

To demonstrate this key point, suppose that with better inventory management the company could have reduced its average inventory holding period to, say, 10 weeks. This would have been a rather dramatic improvement. But modern inventory management techniques such as supply-chain management promise such improvement. If the company had reduced its average inventory holding period to just 10 weeks, its ending inventory would have been:

$$\frac{10}{52} \times \begin{array}{c} \$33,800,000 \\ \text{Cost of Goods Sold} \\ \text{Expense for Year} \end{array} = \begin{array}{c} \$6,500,000 \\ \text{Ending Inventory} \end{array}$$

In this scenario ending inventory would be $1,950,000 less ($8,450,000 versus $6,500,000). The company would have needed $1,950,000 less capital, or would have had this much more cash balance at its disposal.

Caution: With only 10 weeks' inventory, the company may be unable to make some sales because certain products might not be available for immediate delivery to customers. In other words, if overall inventory is too low, stock-outs may occur. Nothing is more frustrating, especially to the sales staff, than having willing customers but no products to deliver to them. The cost of carrying inventory has to be balanced against the profit opportunities lost by not having products on hand ready for sale.

In summary, business managers, creditors, and investors should watch that the inventory holding period is neither too long nor too short. If too long, capital is being wasted; if too short, profit opportunities are being missed. Comparisons of a company's inventory holding period with those of its competitors and with historical trends provide useful benchmarks.

Accounting Issues

Accounting for cost of goods sold expense and the cost of inventory is beset with many problems. First of all, I should mention that businesses that manufacture the products they sell have serious problems in determining the total cost per unit of the different products they produce. Believe me, this is no walk in the park.

College and university accounting programs offer one entire course on this topic (usually called cost accounting). One main problem is the allocation of *indirect* production costs to the different products that benefit from the cost. For example, how should you allocate the cost of security guards who patrol many production departments, or the depreciation on the production plant in which hundreds of different products are manufactured?

Retailers and wholesalers (distributors) buy products in a condition ready for resale. Compared with manufacturers, resellers have a much easier time determining the cost of the products they sell—although there are a few thorny problems. In any case, once acquisition costs have been recorded (for both manufacturers and resellers), another problem rears its ugly head: Product costs fluctuate over time. Period to period, product costs move up or down.

Suppose a business has acquired two units of a product, the first for $100 and the second for $104. The business sells one unit of the product. What is the correct cost to remove from the inventory asset account and to record in cost of goods sold expense? Accountants have come up with three different ways to answer this question: $100 (first-in, first-out); $102 (average cost); and $104 (last-in, first-out). All three methods are acceptable. Different businesses use different methods.

You might think that a business would select the method that gives it the best match with its sales revenue, to get the best measure of gross margin. Generally speaking, the best method would be the one that is most consistent with how the business sets its sales prices. But this logic does not always prevail. A business selects a cost of goods sold method for other reasons, and the method may or may not jibe with its sales pricing policies.

The inventory asset account is written down to record losses from falling sales prices, lower replacement costs, damage and spoilage, and shrinkage (shoplifting and employee theft). The losses may be recorded in the cost of goods sold expense account, or be put in another expense account. Companies do not disclose where the losses from these write-downs are recorded.

Since a business has a choice of accounting methods, it should reveal its cost of goods sold expense method in the footnotes to its financial statements. If the business uses the last-in, first-out method, it should disclose in the footnote the approximate current cost value of its inventory as if it had been using the first-in, first-out method. Other unusual events, such as a major write-down of inventory, also should be disclosed in the footnote. Unfortunately, inventory footnotes are fairly technical and difficult to understand.

EXHIBIT 6.1—INVENTORY AND ACCOUNTS PAYABLE
Dollar Amounts in Thousands

BALANCE SHEET AT YEAR-END

ASSETS

Cash	$ 3,265
Accounts Receivable	5,000
Inventory	8,450
Prepaid Expenses	960
Property, Plant, and Equipment	16,500
Accumulated Depreciation	(4,250)
Intangible Assets	5,575
Total Assets	$35,500

Assuming the amount payable at year-end for inventory-related purchases is four weeks of the 13 weeks in inventory, the year-end balance of Accounts Payable for inventory is:

$$4/13 \times \$8,450 = \$2,600$$

INCOME STATEMENT FOR YEAR

Sales Revenue	$ 52,000
Cost of Goods Sold Expense	(33,800)
Selling, General, and Adm. Expenses	(12,480)
Depreciation Expense	(785)
Interest Expense	(545)
Income Tax Expense	(1,748)
Net Income	$ 2,642

LIABILITIES and STOCKHOLDERS' EQUITY

Accounts Payable	$2,600	
Accounts Payable	720	$ 3,320
Accrued Expenses Payable		1,515
Income Tax Payable		165
Short-Term Notes Payable		3,125
Long-Term Notes Payable		4,250
Capital Stock		8,125
Retained Earnings		15,000
Total Liabilities and Stockholders' Equity		$35,500

6

INVENTORY AND ACCOUNTS PAYABLE

Acquiring Inventory on the Cuff

Please refer to Exhibit 6.1 at the start of the chapter. This chapter focuses on the connection between the *inventory* asset account in the balance sheet and the *accounts payable* liability in the balance sheet. Virtually every business reports accounts payable in its balance sheet, which is a short-term, non-interest-bearing liability arising from buying on credit.

One source of accounts payable is from making *inventory* purchases on credit. A second source of accounts payable is from *expenses* that are not paid immediately. Therefore, at this point I divide the total balance of the company's accounts payable liability into two parts, one for each source (refer to Exhibit 6.1 again).

The previous two chapters connect an income statement account with a balance sheet account. In this chapter we look at a connection between two balance sheet accounts. The linkage explained in this chapter is not about how sales revenue or an expense drives an asset, but rather how inventory drives its corresponding liability.

The company in this example is a manufacturer, which means it makes the products it sells. To begin, the company purchases raw materials needed in its production process. These purchases are made on credit; the company doesn't pay for these purchases right away. Also, other production inputs are bought on credit. For example, once a month the public utility sends a bill for the gas and electricity used during the month, and the company takes several weeks before paying its utility bills. The company purchases several other manufacturing inputs on credit also.

In contrast, retailers and wholesalers (distributors) don't make the products they sell; they buy products in a condition ready for resale. They also make purchases on credit and they have accounts payable from inventory, the same as manufacturers.

In the balance sheet shown in Exhibit 6.1, the company's $2,600,000 liability for its production-related purchases on credit is presented as the first of two accounts payable amounts. The company's selling, general, and administrative expenses also generate accounts payable; the total amount of these unpaid bills ($720,000) is shown as the second accounts payable liability amount (see Exhibit 6.1 again). I discuss the second source of accounts payable in Chapter 7.

The company's inventory holding period is much longer than its purchase credit period (which is typical for most businesses). In other words, accounts payable are paid much sooner than inventory is sold. In this example, the company's inventory holding period from start of the production process to final sale averages 13 weeks (as explained in Chapter 5). But the company pays its accounts payable in four weeks, on average.

Some purchases are paid for quickly, to take advantage of prompt payment discounts offered by vendors. The business takes six weeks or longer to pay many other invoices. Based on its experience and policies, a business knows the average purchase credit period for its production-related purchases. In this example, suppose the business takes four weeks on average to pay these liabilities.

Therefore, the year-end balance of accounts payable for inventory-related purchases on credit can be expressed as follows:

$$\frac{4}{13} \times \begin{array}{c} \$8,450,000 \\ \text{Inventory} \end{array} = \begin{array}{c} \$2,600,000 \\ \text{Accounts Payable} \end{array}$$

In short, this liability equals $\frac{4}{13}$ of the inventory balance. The business gets a free ride for the first four weeks of holding inventory because it waits this long before paying for its purchases on credit. However, the remaining nine weeks of its inventory holding period have to be financed from debt and stockholders' equity sources of capital.

Economists are fond of saying that "there's no such thing as a free lunch." With this in mind, calling the four-week delay in paying for purchases on credit a free ride is not entirely accurate. Sellers that extend credit set their prices slightly higher to compensate for the delay in receiving cash from their customers. In other words, a small but hidden interest charge is built into the cost paid by the purchasers.

Accounting Issues

Several serious accounting issues concerning inventory are discussed at the end of Chapter 5. In sharp contrast, there are relatively few accounting problems as such concerning the accounts payable liability. The main financial reporting issue concerns *disclosure* of relevant information about this liability.

Financial statement readers are entitled to assume that the amount reported for accounts payable is the amount that will be paid in the near future. Suppose, however, that the business is in the middle of negotiations with one or more of its accounts payable creditors regarding prices and other terms. Suppose that these disagreements involve material (significant) amounts. In this situation, the business should make a disclosure about these negotiations in the footnotes to its financial statements.

Also, financial statement readers are entitled to assume that the company's accounts payable creditors (the parties to whom it owes money) do *not* have senior or prior claims ahead of other creditors and debtholders of the business. In other words, the accounts payable creditors are assumed to be *general* creditors of the business, with no special claims on the assets of the business.

If in fact the accounts payable creditors have unusual rights for payment against the business, these abnormal claims should be disclosed in the footnotes to its financial statements.

Here is another important point: Financial statement readers are entitled to assume that the accounts payable are *current*, which means that the liabilities are not seriously overdue (i.e., way beyond their due dates for payment). Suppose, for instance, that half of the company's accounts payable are two or three months overdue. In this situation the business should disclose the overdue amount in the footnotes to its financial statements.

I may not need to emphasize this, but accounts payable are non-interest-bearing and should not be intermingled with the interest-bearing debts of the business. As you see in Exhibit 6.1, interest-bearing liabilities (notes payable) are reported in separate liability accounts. By the way, long-overdue accounts payable may begin to accrue interest at the option of the creditor.

I should mention that the disclosure standards I discuss here for accounts payable are not necessarily complied with in actual financial reports. You don't see much disclosure about accounts payable in business financial statements. I think a business should make full disclosure in its financial reports. But in fact companies are cut a lot of slack in the area of accounts payable. You don't find detailed information about its accounts payable liability in a company's financial statements, even though this particular liability may be more than 10% of a company's total assets and may be larger than its cash balance at the balance sheet date (as it is in our business example).

EXHIBIT 7.1—SELLING, GENERAL, AND ADMINISTRATIVE EXPENSES AND ACCOUNTS PAYABLE

Dollar Amounts in Thousands

BALANCE SHEET AT YEAR-END

ASSETS

Cash	$ 3,265
Accounts Receivable	5,000
Inventory	8,450
Prepaid Expenses	960
Property, Plant, and Equipment	16,500
Accumulated Depreciation	(4,250)
Intangible Assets	5,575
Total Assets	$35,500

INCOME STATEMENT FOR YEAR

Sales Revenue	$ 52,000
Cost of Goods Sold Expense	(33,800)
Selling, General, and Adm. Expenses	(12,480)
Depreciation Expense	(785)
Interest Expense	(545)
Income Tax Expense	(1,748)
Net Income	$ 2,642

> Assuming three weeks of annual selling, general, and administrative expenses are unpaid at the end of the year, the year-end balance of Accounts Payable for these unpaid expenses is:
>
> $3/52 \times \$12,480 = \$720$

LIABILITIES and STOCKHOLDERS' EQUITY

Accounts Payable	$2,600	
Accounts Payable	720	$ 3,320
Accrued Expenses Payable		1,515
Income Tax Payable		165
Short-Term Notes Payable		3,125
Long-Term Notes Payable		4,250
Capital Stock		8,125
Retained Earnings		15,000
Total Liabilities and Stockholders' Equity		$35,500

7

OPERATING EXPENSES AND ACCOUNTS PAYABLE

Recording Expenses Before They Are Paid

Please refer to Exhibit 7.1 at the start of the chapter, which highlights the connection between *selling, general, and administrative expenses* in the income statement and the second of the two *accounts payable* components in the balance sheet. Recall from Chapter 6 the two sources of accounts payable—from inventory purchases on credit, and from expenses not paid immediately. Chapter 6 explains the connection between inventory and accounts payable. This chapter explains how expenses drive the accounts payable liability of a business.

Every business in the world has a wide variety of *operating* expenses. The term "operating" does *not* include cost of goods sold, interest, and income tax expenses. Also, in our example, the company's depreciation expense is reported separately. All other operating expenses are combined into one conglomerate account labeled "Selling, General, and Administrative Expenses" (see the income statement in Exhibit 7.1). This expense title is widely used by businesses, although you see variations of this title.

Day in and day out, many operating expenses are recorded when they are paid, at which time an expense account is increased and the cash account is decreased. But some operating expenses have to be recorded *before* they are paid—which is the focus of this chapter.

"Operating expenses" is the convenient term I use in the collective sense to refer to many different specific expenses of running (operating) a business enterprise. In this business example, the annual depreciation expense on the company's long-lived,

fixed assets is shown as a separate expense. So, the $12,480,000 total of selling, general, and administrative expenses does not include depreciation. (It would if the depreciation expense were not reported separately.) And, to remind you, the $12,480,000 total for operating expenses does not include cost of goods sold, interest, and income tax expenses, which are reported separately in the income statement (see Exhibit 7.1).

Operating expenses include the following specific expenses (in no particular order):

- Rental of buildings, copiers, computers, telephone system equipment, and other assets.

- Wages, salaries, commissions, bonuses, and other compensation paid to managers, office staff, salespersons, warehouse workers, security guards, and other employees. (Compensation of production employees is included in the cost of goods manufactured and becomes part of inventory cost.)

- Payroll taxes and fringe benefit costs of labor, such as health and medical plan contributions and the cost of employee retirement plans (a very difficult cost to measure for defined benefit plans).

- Office and data processing supplies.

- Telephone, fax, Internet, and web site costs.

- Inventory shrinkage due to shoplifting and employee theft or careless handling and storage of products; the cost of goods stolen and damaged may be written off to cost of goods sold expense or, alternatively, classified as an operating expense.

+ Liability, fire, accident, and other insurance costs.

+ Utility costs of electricity and fuel.

+ Advertising and sales promotion costs, which are major expenditures by many businesses.

+ Bad debts, which are past-due accounts receivable that turn out to be not collectible and have to be written off.

+ Transportation and shipping costs.

+ Travel and entertainment costs.

This list is not all-inclusive. I'm sure you could think of many more expenses of operating a business. Even relatively small businesses keep 100 or more separate accounts for specific operating expenses. Larger business corporations keep thousands of specific expense accounts. In their external financial reports, however, most publicly owned corporations report only one, two, or three operating expenses. For instance, advertising expenses are reported internally to managers, but you don't see this particular expense in many external income statements.

Some operating expenses are recorded when they are paid—not before, nor after. The business records an expense and decreases cash. This chapter focuses on another basic way that operating expenses are recorded—by increasing the accounts payable liability. (Following chapters explain the other ways of recording operating expenses and the asset and liability accounts involved.)

It would be convenient if every dollar of operating expenses were a dollar actually paid out in the same period. But business is not so simple, as this and later chapters demonstrate. The point is that for many operating expenses a business cannot wait to record the expense until it pays the expense. As soon as a liability is incurred, the amount of expense has to be recorded.

A liability is incurred when a company takes on an obligation to make future payment and has received the economic benefit of the cost in operating the business. Recording the liability for an unpaid expense is one fundamental aspect of *accrual-basis accounting*. Expenses are *accrued* (i.e., recorded before they are paid) so that the amount of each expense is deducted from sales revenue in order to measure profit correctly for the period.

For example, suppose on December 15 a business receives an invoice from its attorneys for legal work done for the company over the previous two or three months. The end of the company's accounting (fiscal) year is December 31. The company will not pay its lawyers until next year. This cost belongs in this year, and should be recorded in the legal expense account. Therefore, the company records an increase in the accounts payable liability account to record the legal expense.

This is just one example of many; other examples include bills from newspapers for advertisements that have already appeared in the papers, telephone bills, and so on. Generally speaking, liabilities for unpaid expenses are for short credit periods, typically one month or less.

Based on its experience, a business should know the average time it takes to pay its short-term accounts payable arising from unpaid operating expenses. The average credit period of the company in our example is three weeks. Thus, the amount of its accounts payable from this source can be expressed as follows:

$$\frac{3}{52} \times \begin{array}{c} \$12,480,000 \\ \text{Operating Expenses} \\ \text{for Year} \end{array} = \begin{array}{c} \$720,000 \\ \text{Accounts} \\ \text{Payable} \end{array}$$

In Exhibit 7.1 note that the year-end amount for this component of accounts payable is $720,000.

Operating costs that are not paid immediately are recorded in the accounts payable liability account both to recognize the obligation of the business to make payment for these costs, and to record expenses that have benefited the operations of the business so that profit is measured correctly for the period. In other words, there is both an income statement and a balance sheet reason for recording unpaid expenses.

There's no question that accounts payable should be recorded for expenses that haven't been paid by the end of the accounting year. However, the recording of unpaid expenses does not decrease cash. Actual cash outflow occurs later, when the accounts payable are paid. Chapter 13 examines the cash flow aspects of making profit.

Accounting Issues

At the end of Chapter 6 I discuss the accounting issues regarding reporting accounts payable in the balance sheet. You may want to quickly review those points.

Generally speaking, there are no accounting problems regarding the accounts payable liability for unpaid operating expenses. The amounts that should be recorded are pretty clear in most situations. The business receives invoices (bills) for these expenses that are definite regarding the amounts owed by the business. Some of its vendors and suppliers may offer prompt payment discounts. For example, the business may deduct 2% if it pays the bill in 10 days or sooner. Generally, a business adopts a standard way of dealing with such discounts and follows the method consistently.

The most contentious financial reporting issue concerns disclosure of operating expenses in a company's income statement. Suppose you were one of the stockholders in the business. Would you be satisfied with the company disclosing only one grand total for all its selling, general, and administrative expenses, as in Exhibit 2.2? Or would you want more detail?

In later chapters I discuss the broad issue of adequate disclosure in financial reports. All I'll say here is that financial reporting standards are not very demanding regarding disclosure of expenses in income statements to share owners. Companies can be tight-lipped if they so choose.

EXHIBIT 8.1—SELLING, GENERAL, AND ADMINISTRATIVE EXPENSES AND PREPAID EXPENSES

Dollar Amounts in Thousands

INCOME STATEMENT FOR YEAR

Sales Revenue	$ 52,000
Cost of Goods Sold Expense	(33,800)
Selling, General, and Adm. Expenses	(12,480)
Depreciation Expense	(785)
Interest Expense	(545)
Income Tax Expense	(1,748)
Net Income	$ 2,642

Assuming the business has paid certain costs that will not be recorded as expenses until next year that in total equal four weeks of its annual operating expenses, the year-end balance of Prepaid Expenses is:

$$4/52 \times \$12,480 = \$960$$

BALANCE SHEET AT YEAR-END

ASSETS

Cash	$ 3,265
Accounts Receivable	5,000
Inventory	8,450
Prepaid Expenses	960
Property, Plant, and Equipment	16,500
Accumulated Depreciation	(4,250)
Intangible Assets	5,575
Total Assets	$35,500

LIABILITIES and STOCKHOLDERS' EQUITY

Accounts Payable	$ 3,320
Accrued Expenses Payable	1,515
Income Tax Payable	165
Short-Term Notes Payable	3,125
Long-Term Notes Payable	4,250
Capital Stock	8,125
Retained Earnings	15,000
Total Liabilities and Stockholders' Equity	$35,500

8

OPERATING EXPENSES AND PREPAID EXPENSES

Paying Certain Operating Costs Before
They Are Recorded as Expenses

Please refer to Exhibit 8.1 at the start of the chapter, which highlights the connection between *selling, general, and administrative expenses* in the income statement and the *prepaid expenses* asset account in the balance sheet. This chapter explains that operating expenses drive this particular asset of a business.

The preceding chapter explains that some operating expenses are recorded before they are paid—by recording a liability for the unpaid expenses. This chapter, in contrast, explains that certain operating costs are paid *before* the amounts should be recorded as expenses.

Insurance premiums are one example of prepaid expenses. Insurance premiums are paid in advance of the insurance policy period—which usually extends over 6 or 12 months. Another example is office and computer supplies bought in bulk and then gradually used up over several weeks or months. Annual property taxes may be paid at the start of the tax year; these amounts should be allocated over the future months that benefit from the property taxes.

Cash outlays for prepaid costs are initially put in the *prepaid expenses* asset account that acts as a holding account, and then the amounts are gradually charged out over time to operating expenses. This two-step process is the means of delaying the expensing of costs to future periods. The prepaid cost is allocated so that each future month receives its fair share of the cost. When

the time comes, an entry is recorded to remove the appropriate portion of the cost from the prepaid expenses asset account, and the amount is entered in an operating expense account.

Based on its experience and the nature of its operations, a business knows how large, on average, the total of its prepaid expenses is relative to its annual operating expenses. In this example the company's prepaid expenses equal four weeks of its annual operating expenses. Thus, the balance in its prepaid expenses asset account can be expressed as follows:

$$\frac{4}{52} \times \begin{array}{c} \$12{,}480{,}000 \text{ Selling,} \\ \text{General, and Administrative} \\ \text{Expenses for Year} \end{array} = \begin{array}{c} \$960{,}000 \\ \text{Prepaid} \\ \text{Expenses} \end{array}$$

In Exhibit 8.1, notice that the year-end balance of this asset account is $960,000, which is much smaller than the company's accounts receivable and inventory assets. (This is typical for most businesses.)

Summing up, the main reason for recording operating costs that are paid in advance in the prepaid expenses asset account is to delay recording these costs as expenses until the proper time. Charging off prepayments immediately to expenses would be premature—it would be robbing Paul (expenses higher this period) to pay Peter (expenses lower next period).

The main purpose of putting prepaid operating costs into the prepaid expenses account is not to recognize an asset, although prepaid costs are a legitimate asset. In one sense, prepaying an operating expense is similar to making an investment in a long-term operating asset such as a building, or equipment and machinery.

Charging off prepaid operating costs to expenses is done over a short time, whereas allocating the cost of a building to expense is spread out over many years (as the next chapter explains).

The prepayment of operating expenses decreases cash, of course. Cash outflow takes place sooner than the expense is recorded. Chapter 13 explains the cash flow analysis of expenses and sales revenue.

Accounting Issues

In the large majority of situations there are no serious accounting problems concerning prepaid expenses. However, I can imagine an unusual situation in which the balance in a company's prepaid expenses asset account should be written down as a loss. For instance, a business may be on the verge of collapse, and its prepaid expenses may therefore have no future benefit and may not be recoverable.

I haven't said much about *accounting fraud* and *massaging the numbers* so far in the book. This is as good a place as any to open up the discussion of these dark corners of accounting. As you probably know, some businesses deliberately distort the recording of their expenses and sales revenue, in order to hide financial problems or to inflate profit. Prepaid expenses, being a relatively small asset, are not an important element in accounting fraud. (I discuss the serious problems of accounting fraud in Chapters 20 and 21.)

The prepaid expenses account can be used to massage the numbers in order to hold down or to pump up the amount of operating expenses recorded in the period. For example, a business may not record prepaid costs; instead it could simply record the prepayments immediately to expense. Alternatively, a business could intentionally delay charging off certain prepaid costs to expenses, even though the expenses should be recorded in this period.

Accountants do not take the initiative on their own when massaging the numbers. A top-level manager, either directly or indirectly, instructs the accountant to come up with more (or less) profit for the period—by whatever means it takes. In doing so the accountant has to override established accounting procedures. Needless to say, this puts the accountant in an ethical dilemma. Also, the CPA auditor of the company's financial statements should discover any significant amount of accounting manipulation. The auditor has to decide what to do about it (see Chapter 21).

I discuss accounting fraud and massaging the numbers further in Chapters 20 and 21. I should point out here, however, that massaging the numbers for sales revenue and expenses affects both the income statement *and* the balance sheet. Manipulating the accounting numbers has a double-edged effect—both the income statement and the balance sheet include wrong amounts.

Suppose, for instance, that some of the products in the company's ending inventory suffered uninsured damage during the year. The damaged products will be sold next year below cost.

Accounting theory is clear: The loss should be recorded in the period the damage occurs. But top management wants to record the hit against profit this year. The loss can be more easily absorbed next year (they think).

So, the accountant does not record the loss this year. Therefore, bottom-line profit in the income statement is too high. And, the amount of inventory in the balance sheet at the end of the year is too high. Also, the retained earnings account in the balance sheet (which accumulates the profit recorded each year) is too high. Both financial statements contain deliberate errors.

Needless to say, business managers and accountants should have ethical qualms about massaging the numbers. But I can say without fear of contradiction that manipulating the accounting numbers goes on all the time. As I say earlier, this is a dark corner of accounting.

EXHIBIT 9.1—PROPERTY, PLANT, AND EQUIPMENT; DEPRECIATION EXPENSE; AND ACCUMULATED DEPRECIATION

Dollar Amounts in Thousands

BALANCE SHEET AT YEAR-END

ASSETS

Cash		$ 3,265
Accounts Receivable		5,000
Inventory		8,450
Prepaid Expenses		960
Property, Plant, and Equipment	$16,500	
Accumulated Depreciation	(4,250)	12,250
Intangible Assets		5,575
Total Assets		$35,500

> The costs of long-term operating assets (except land) are allocated to depreciation expense over the years of their estimated useful lives.

> The amount of depreciation expense is not recorded as a decrease in the asset account. Instead it is accumulated in a *contra* or *offset* account, called Accumulated Depreciation.

INCOME STATEMENT FOR YEAR

Sales Revenue	$ 52,000
Cost of Goods Sold Expense	(33,800)
Selling, General, and Adm. Expenses	(12,480)
Depreciation Expense	(785)
Interest Expense	(545)
Income Tax Expense	(1,748)
Net Income	$ 2,642

LIABILITIES and STOCKHOLDERS' EQUITY

Accounts Payable	$ 3,320
Accrued Expenses Payable	1,515
Income Tax Payable	165
Short-Term Notes Payable	3,125
Long-Term Notes Payable	4,250
Capital Stock	8,125
Retained Earnings	15,000
Total Liabilities and Stockholders' Equity	$35,500

9

A UNIQUE EXPENSE: DEPRECIATION

Brief Review of Expense Accounting

By now you should have a basic sense of *accrual-based* expense accounting. Cash outlays for operating a business are not necessarily recorded to expense in the same period the cash disbursement takes place. In other words, expenses are not recorded on a simple *cash basis* of accounting, where all a business needs to do is to keep track of the checks it writes.

Rather, financial statement accounting is concerned with the correct *timing* for recording expenses—to match expenses with sales revenue or to match expenses with the correct period if there is no direct association between a particular expense and sales revenue. These two guiding principles for recording expenses are explained briefly as follows:

- *Matching Expenses with Sales Revenue:* Cost of goods sold expense, sales commissions expense, and any other expense directly connected with making particular sales are recorded in the same period as the sales revenue. This is straightforward; all direct expenses of making sales should be matched against sales revenue. You agree, don't you?

- *Matching Expenses with the Correct Period:* Many expenses are not directly identifiable with particular sales, such as office employees' salaries, rental of warehouse space, computer processing and accounting costs, legal and audit fees, interest on borrowed money, and many more. Nondirect expenses are just as necessary as direct expenses. But nondirect expenses cannot be matched with particular sales. Therefore, nondirect expenses are recorded in the period in which the benefit to the business occurs.

Recall that the recording of expenses involves the use of asset and liability accounts. Chapter 5 explains the use of the inventory account to hold the cost of products that are manufactured or purchased until the goods are sold, at which time cost of goods expense is recorded. Chapter 7 explains the use of the accounts payable liability account for unpaid costs that should be recorded as expenses in the period. Chapter 8 explains the use of the prepaid expenses asset account to delay recording operating expenses until the proper time period.

This chapter explains that the costs of the long-lived operating assets of a business are spread out over their useful lives. The allocation of the cost of a long-term operating asset to expense is called *depreciation*. Please be careful: Many persons think depreciation refers to the loss of value, or decline in market value of an asset such as a personal automobile. This notion is not entirely wrong, but in financial statement accounting depreciation means *cost allocation*.

Depreciation Expense

Please refer to Exhibit 9.1 at the start of the chapter, which shows the connections between *property, plant, and equipment* in the balance sheet and *depreciation expense* in the income statement, and from depreciation expense to the *accumulated depreciation* account in the balance sheet. In brief, the costs of the company's long-term operating assets are allocated over their estimated economic lives, and the annual depreciation expense is accumulated in a separate contra (offset) account that is deducted from the cost of the assets. The logic and methods of recording depreciation expense are explained in this chapter.

The company in this example needs certain specialized machinery, equipment, and tools that are rented under multiyear lease contracts. Legally the business doesn't own leased assets. The monthly rents paid on these leases are charged to expenses. Leased assets are not reported in a company's balance sheet (unless the lease is essentially a method to finance the purchase of the asset). The company discloses rent payment commitments of long-term leases in the footnotes to its financial statements.

The company in our example owns long-term operating assets—a production plant and office building, furniture and fixtures, computers, delivery trucks, forklifts, and automobiles used by its salespersons. The business buys these assets, uses them for several years, and eventually disposes of them. Because of their long-term nature, accountants call them *fixed assets*, although this term is hardly ever used in the formal financial statements of a business.

The long-term operating assets owned by a business usually are grouped into one inclusive account for balance sheet reporting. One common title is "Property, Plant, and Equipment," which I use. (A detailed breakdown of fixed assets may be disclosed in a footnote to the financial statements, or in a separate schedule.) At the end of its most recent year, the business reports that the total cost of its fixed assets (property, plant, and equipment) is $16,500,000—see Exhibit 9.1. This amount is the total of the original costs of its fixed assets, or how much they cost when the business bought them.

Fixed assets are used for several years, but eventually they wear out or lose their utility to a business. In short, these assets have a limited life span—they don't last forever. For example, delivery trucks may be driven 200,000 or 300,000 miles, but are replaced eventually.

The cost of a delivery truck, for instance, is prorated over the years of expected use to the business. How many years, exactly? A business has its experience to go on in estimating the useful lives of fixed assets. In theory, a business should make the most realistic forecast possible regarding how long each fixed asset will be used, and then spread the asset's cost over this life span. However, theory doesn't count for much on this score. Most businesses turn to the federal income tax code and regulations for the useful lives of their fixed assets, because these lives are permitted for calculating the deductible depreciation amounts in their federal income tax returns.

In the federal income tax system, every kind of fixed asset is given a minimum life over which its cost can be depreciated. The cost of land is not depreciated, on grounds that land never wears out and has a perpetual life. (Of course, the market value of a parcel of real estate can fluctuate over time; and land can be destroyed by floods and earthquakes—but that's another matter.)

The federal income tax permits (but does not require) *accelerated depreciation* methods. The term "accelerated" means two different things. First, for income tax, fixed assets can be depreciated over lives that are considerably *shorter* than their actual useful lives. For example, automobiles and light trucks can be depreciated over five years even though these fixed assets typically last longer than five years (except perhaps taxicabs in New York City). Buildings placed in service after 1993 can be depreciated over 39 years, but most buildings stand longer. In writing the income tax law, Congress decided that allowing businesses to depreciate their fixed assets faster than they actually wear out is good economic policy.

Second, "accelerated" means *front-loaded*; more of the cost of a fixed asset is depreciated in the first half of its useful life than in its second half. Instead of a level, uniform amount of depreciation expense year to year (which is called the *straight-line* method), the income tax law allows a business to deduct higher amounts of depreciation expense in the front (first) years and less in the back (later) years.

A business can reduce its taxable income in the early years of its fixed assets by choosing accelerated depreciation methods. But these effects don't necessarily mean it's the best depreciation method in theory or in actual practice. Nevertheless, accelerated depreciation methods, given the imprimatur of the income tax code, are very popular.

A business must maintain a depreciation schedule for each of its fixed assets and keep track of original cost and how much depreciation expense is recorded each year. Only cost can be depreciated. Once the total cost of a fixed asset has been depreciated, no more depreciation expense can be recorded. At this point, the fixed asset is fully depreciated even though it still may be used several more years.

In our company example, the depreciation expense for its most recent year is $785,000—see Exhibit 9.1. Its manufacturing and office building is being depreciated by the straight-line method; its other fixed assets (e.g., trucks, computers, equipment) are being depreciated according to an accelerated method.

The amount of depreciation expense charged to each year is quite arbitrary compared with most other operating expenses. The main reason is that useful life estimates are arbitrary. For a six-month insurance policy, there's little doubt that the total premium cost should be allocated over exactly six months. But long-lived operating assets such as office desks, display shelving, file cabinets, computers, and so on present much more difficult problems. Past experience is a good guide but leaves much room for error.

Given the inherent problems of estimating useful lives, financial statement readers are well advised to keep in mind the consequences of adopting ultraconservative useful life estimates. If useful life estimates are too short (the assets are actually used many more years), then depreciation expense is recorded too quickly. Keep this point in mind.

A business could keep two sets of depreciation books. It could depreciate fixed assets over short lives for income tax, and use longer, more realistic lives for financial reporting. However, most businesses use the income tax depreciation lives in their financial statements. Rapid (accelerated) depreciation is the norm.

Every expense is either a decrease in an asset or an increase in a liability. Recording depreciation expense does *not*—I repeat, does *not*—decrease cash; cash is not involved in recording depreciation. Rather, recording depreciation expense has the effect of decreasing a fixed asset. To understand this point, you have to understand the accumulated depreciation account, which I explain next.

Accumulated Depreciation and Book Value of Fixed Assets

The amount of depreciation each period is *not* recorded as decreases in the fixed asset accounts. Yet, decreasing the asset account would seem to make sense because the whole point of depreciation is to recognize the wearing out of the fixed asset over time. So, why not decrease the fixed asset account?

Well, the universal practice throughout the accounting world is to accumulate depreciation expense in a companion account called *accumulated depreciation*. This account does what its name implies—it accumulates, period by period, the amounts recorded as depreciation expense. In Exhibit 9.1, notice that the balance in this account at the end of the company's most recent year is $4,250,000.

Compared to the $16,500,000 cost of its fixed assets, the accumulated depreciation balance indicates that the company's fixed assets are not very old. Furthermore, the company recorded $785,000 depreciation expense in its most recent year. At this clip, a little more than five years' depreciation has been recorded on its property, plant, and equipment (fixed assets).

As you see in Exhibit 9.1, the balance in accumulated depreciation is deducted from the original cost of fixed assets. In our business example, the $16,500,000 cost of fixed assets less the $4,250,000 accumulated depreciation equals $12,250,000. Cost less accumulated depreciation is called the *book value* of fixed assets.

Generally the entire cost of a fixed asset is depreciated, assuming the business holds on to the asset until the end of its depreciation life. In one sense, book value represents future depreciation expense, although a business may dispose of some of its fixed assets before they are fully depreciated. (And keep in mind that the cost of land, which is included in the property, plant, and equipment account, is not depreciated.)

Finally, keep in mind that the $4,250,000 accumulated depreciation balance is the total depreciation that has been recorded during all years the fixed assets have been used. It's not just the depreciation expense from the most recent year.

Book Values and Current Replacement Values

After recording depreciation expense for its most recent year, the book value of the company's long-term operating (fixed) assets is $12,250,000 (see Exhibit 9.1). Suppose that the business could determine the current market replacement costs at the balance sheet date of the same exact fixed assets in the same used condition. (Of course, this might not be possible.)

Would you expect that the current market replacement cost would equal the book value of the fixed assets? Chances are that the current market replacement costs would be higher than the book value of the fixed assets—due to general inflation and the use of accelerated depreciation methods.

The original costs of fixed assets reported in a balance sheet are not meant to be indicators of the current replacement costs of the assets. Original costs are the amounts of capital invested in the assets that should be recovered through sales revenue over the years from using the assets in the operations of the business. Depreciation accounting is a cost-recovery-based method—not a "mark-to-market" method. In short, fixed assets accounting does not attempt to record changes in current replacement cost.

I should point out that business managers shouldn't ignore the current replacement values of their fixed assets. Fixed assets can be destroyed or damaged by fire, flooding, riots, terrorist acts, tornadoes, explosions, and structural failure. Quite clearly, business managers should be concerned about insuring fixed assets for their current replacement costs. However, for financial reporting purposes a business does not write up the recorded value of its fixed assets to reflect current replacement costs.

You see criticism of financial statement accounting on grounds that depreciation expense is based on the historical cost of fixed assets—instead of current replacement costs. Someday Congress might consider changing the income tax law to allow replacement-cost-basis depreciation (without taxing the gain from writing up fixed assets to their higher replacement costs). I don't see any evidence of Congress making such a fundamental change in the federal income tax law.

I must admit, though, that anything is possible regarding fixed-asset depreciation within the federal income tax law. For instance, I would not be surprised if Congress were to change the useful lives of fixed assets for business income tax purposes—which Congress has done in the past. But Congress has not been willing to abandon the cost basis for fixed-asset depreciation.

Intangible Assets

So far in the chapter I have focused on the depreciation of *tangible* fixed assets. Many businesses invest in *intangible* assets, which have no physical existence. You can't see or touch these assets. For example, a business may purchase a valuable patent that it will use in its production process over many years. Or a business may buy an established trademark that is well known among consumers. When a business buys patents or trademarks, the costs of these particular assets are recorded in long-term asset accounts called "Patents" and "Trademarks."

A business may purchase another going business as a whole and pay more than the sum of its identifiable assets (minus its liabilities). Often the company to be acquired has been in business for many years and it has built up a trusted name and reputation. It may have a large list of loyal customers that will continue to buy the company's products in the future. The experience and loyalty of the acquired company's employees may be the main reason to pay for more than the identifiable assets being acquired in the purchase of the business. Or the business being bought out may have secret processes and product formulas that give it a strong competitive advantage.

There are many reasons to pay more for an established, going-concern business than just the sum of its identifiable assets (minus the liabilities being assumed by buying the other business).

When a business pays more than the sum of the specific assets (less liabilities) of the business being acquired, the excess is generally recorded in the asset account called *goodwill*. Whether to systematically charge off the cost of goodwill and other intangible assets has been a vexing issue over the years. I won't bore you here with a technical discussion of the various arguments.

At the present time, accounting standards do not require the systematic allocation of the cost of an intangible asset to expense (called *amortization* expense). Instead, when an intangible asset has suffered an observable loss of value, a business makes an entry to *write down* the recorded value of the intangible asset. Businesses make yearly assessments of whether their intangible assets have been impaired and, if so, record an expense for the effect of the impairment.

Based on its yearly assessment, the business in our example determined that its intangible assets did not suffer a loss of value during the year. Therefore it did not record an expense for its intangible assets. Notice in Exhibit 9.1 that there is no line of connection from the intangible assets account in the balance sheet to an expense in the income statement. Keep in mind, however, that an expense is recorded when there is a diminishment in value of a company's intangible assets.

Accounting Issues

There's a multitude of accounting problems regarding the depreciation of long-term operating assets, as well as other accounting problems concerning fixed assets. A company's fixed assets are typically a sizable part of its total assets, so these accounting problems are important.

Many books have been written on the theory of depreciation, arguing the merits of different methods. As I mention in the chapter, most businesses adopt the income tax ground rules for depreciating their fixed assets. This is a practical and expedient answer to depreciation accounting questions.

In addition to depreciation, a business should write down fixed assets if their economic value has become impaired. An airline, for example, could have surplus jets that it no longer needs, or a manufacturer may shut down an entire plant because of a fall-off in demand for the products made in the plant. When a business has excess capacity, it should take a hard look at whether its fixed assets should be written down. Making write-downs of fixed assets due to loss of economic value is painful, and can put a big dent in profit, of course.

There are accounting problems in drawing the line between the costs of routine maintenance of fixed assets, which should be expensed as you go, versus major outlays that extend the life or improve the appearance or efficiency of fixed assets. The costs of major improvements should be recorded in the fixed asset account and depreciated over future years.

Seismic shifts in the business environment could justify a company making major changes in its depreciation policies, although you don't see this happening very often. A business may self-insure some of its fixed assets, instead of buying casualty insurance coverage, making it vulnerable to huge write-offs if it suffers an actual loss. When a business self-insures its fixed assets, should it record an estimated expense each year for a future loss that hasn't yet happened, and may never happen?

In summary, there are many serious accounting problems surrounding fixed assets. Therefore, a business definitely should explain its depreciation and other fixed asset accounting policies in the footnotes to its financial statements. Also, a company should disclose how it accounts for its intangible assets, especially when it makes a major write-down in one or more of these assets during the year.

In Chapter 5 I argue that the company's cost of goods sold expense accounting method should be consistent with how the business sets sales prices. Sales revenue has to recover the cost of products sold, of course. Likewise, I would argue that choosing the depreciation expense method should be guided mainly by the number of years over which the business plans to recoup the costs invested in its fixed assets.

As I say earlier in the chapter, most businesses adopt the shortest depreciation lives permitted under the income tax law, regardless of the sales revenue life span of the fixed assets. If the business adopts a sales pricing policy for recapturing the cost of a fixed asset over, say, 20 years, I would argue that a 20-year depreciation life should be used. But it may depreciate the cost over 10 years, as permitted by the income tax law. Talk about a mismatch between sales revenue and expenses!

EXHIBIT 10.1—ACCRUING UNPAID EXPENSES

Dollar Amounts in Thousands

BALANCE SHEET AT YEAR-END

ASSETS

Cash	$ 3,265
Accounts Receivable	5,000
Inventory	8,450
Prepaid Expenses	960
Property, Plant, and Equipment	16,500
Accumulated Depreciation	(4,250)
Intangible Assets	5,575
Total Assets	$35,500

INCOME STATEMENT FOR YEAR

Sales Revenue	$ 52,000
Cost of Goods Sold Expense	(33,800)
Selling, General, and Adm. Expenses	(12,480)
Depreciation Expense	(785)
Interest Expense	(545)
Income Tax Expense	(1,748)
Net Income	$ 2,642

Assuming six weeks of the year's total of selling, general, and administrative expenses is unpaid at year-end, the amount payable for these operating expenses is: 6/52 × $12,480 = $1,440

A small amount of the annual interest expense is unpaid at year-end, which is recorded to recognize the full amount of interest expense for the year.

LIABILITIES and STOCKHOLDERS' EQUITY

Accounts Payable		$ 3,320
Accrued Expenses Payable	$1,440	
Accrued Expenses Payable	75	1,515
Income Tax Payable		165
Short-Term Notes Payable		3,125
Long-Term Notes Payable		4,250
Capital Stock		8,125
Retained Earnings		15,000
Total Liabilities and Stockholders' Equity		$35,500

10

ACCRUING THE LIABILITY FOR UNPAID EXPENSES

Recording the Accrued Liability
for Operating Expenses

Please refer to Exhibit 10.1 at the start of the chapter, which highlights the connections between *selling, general, and administrative expenses* in the income statement and the *accrued expenses payable* liability in the balance sheet, and between *interest expense* in the income statement and the same liability in the balance sheet. You get two for the price of one in this chapter. Both connections are based on the same idea—unpaid expenses at year-end are recorded so that the full, correct amount of expense is recognized in measuring profit for the year.

Chapter 7 explains that a business records certain expenses as soon as the bills (invoices) are received for these operating costs, even though it doesn't pay the bills until weeks later. This chapter explains that a business has to go looking for certain unpaid expenses at the end of the period. No bills or invoices are received for these expenses; they build up, or *accrue* over time.

For instance, the business in our example pays its salespersons commissions based on their sales each month. Commissions are calculated at the end of each month, but are not paid until the following month. At year-end, the sales commissions earned for the final month of the year have not been paid. To record this expense, the company makes an entry in a liability account, called *accrued expenses payable*, which is a different sort of liability than accounts payable.

The accountant should know which expenses accumulate over time and make the appropriate calculations for these unpaid amounts at year-end. A business does not receive an invoice (bill) for these expenses from an outside vendor or supplier. A business has to generate its own internal invoices to itself, as it were. Its accounting department must be especially alert to which specific expenses need to be accrued.

In addition to sales commissions payable, a business has several other accrued expenses that should be recorded at the end of the period; the following are typical examples:

- Accumulated vacation and sick leave pay owed to employees, which can add up to a sizable amount.

- Partial-month telephone and electricity costs that have been incurred but not yet billed to the company.

- Property taxes that should be charged to the year, but the business has not received the tax bill by the end of the year.

- Warranty and guarantee work on products already sold that will be done in the future; the sales revenue has been recorded this year, so these post-sale expenses also should be recorded in the same period to match all expenses with sales revenue.

Failure to record accrued liabilities for unpaid expenses could cause serious errors in a company's annual financial statements—liabilities would be understated in its balance sheet and expenses would be understated in its income statement for the year. A business definitely should identify which expenses accumulate over time and record the appropriate amounts of these liabilities at the end of the year.

In this example, the company's average gestation period before paying certain of its operating expenses is six weeks. Thus, the amount of its accrued expenses payable at the end of the year can be expressed as follows:

$$\frac{6}{52} \times \begin{array}{c} \$12{,}480{,}000 \text{ Selling,} \\ \text{General, and Administrative} \\ \text{Expenses for Year} \end{array} = \begin{array}{c} \$1{,}440{,}000 \\ \text{Accrued Expenses} \\ \text{Payable} \end{array}$$

See in Exhibit 10.1 that the ending balance of accrued expenses payable includes $1,440,000 for operating expenses. Is six weeks right for a typical business? Well, it's difficult to generalize from business to business. I'd say that six weeks is more or less average, but keep in mind that every business is different.

I might mention that it is not unusual that the ending balance of a company's accrued expenses payable is larger than its accounts payable for unpaid operating expenses. In our business example, the ending balance of its accounts payable for operating expenses is $720,000 (from Exhibit 7.1), which is only half as much as its $1,440,000 accrued expenses payable at the end of the year.

Speaking of accounts payable, some businesses merge accrued expenses payable with accounts payable and report only one liability in their external balance sheets. Both types of liabilities are non-interest-bearing. Both emerge out of the operations of the business, and from manufacturing or purchasing products. For this reason they are sometimes called *spontaneous liabilities*, which means they arise on the spot, not from borrowing money but from operating the business. Grouping both types of liabilities in one account is acceptable under financial reporting standards, although they can be reported separately.

The sum of its ending $720,000 accounts payable for operating expenses and its $1,440,000 accrued expenses payable equals $2,160,000. This means the business was relieved of paying this much cash during the year for its operating expenses. (Of course, the money will have to be paid next year.) The sizes of accounts payable and accrued expenses have significant impacts on cash flow, which I explain in Chapter 13. Any change in the size of either of these two liabilities has cash flow impacts that are important to understand.

Bringing Interest Expense Up to Snuff

Virtually all businesses have liabilities for accounts payable and accrued expenses payable—which are part and parcel of carrying on its operations. And most businesses borrow money from a bank or from other sources that lend money to businesses. A note or similar legal instrument is signed when borrowing; hence, the basic liability account is called *notes payable*. Interest is paid on borrowed money, of course, whereas no interest is paid on accounts payable (unless the amount is seriously past due and an interest penalty is added by the creditor). Notes payable always are reported separately and not mixed with non-interest-bearing liabilities.

Interest is a charge per day for the use of borrowed money. Each and every day that money is borrowed increases the amount of interest owed to the lender. The ratio of interest to the amount borrowed is called the *interest rate*, and is stated as a percent. Percent means "per hundred." If you borrow $100,000 for one year and pay $6,000 interest for the use of the money for one year, the interest rate is:

$6,000 Interest ÷ $100,000 Borrowed
= $6 per $100, or 6.0% Annual Interest Rate

Interest rates are stated as annual rates, even though the term of a loan can be shorter or longer than one year.

Interest is reported as a separate expense in income statements. It's not the size of the interest expense, but rather the special nature of interest that requires separate disclosure. Interest is a *financial* expense, as opposed to operating expenses. Interest depends on how the business is financed, which refers to the company's mix of capital sources. The basic choice is between debt capital and equity (the generic term for all kinds of ownership capital).

You may ask: When is interest paid? It depends. On short-term notes (one year or less), interest is commonly paid in one amount at the maturity date of the note, which is the last day of the loan period, at which time the amount borrowed and the accumulated interest are due. On long-term notes payable (longer than one year), interest is paid semiannually, or possibly monthly or quarterly. In any case, on both short-term and long-term notes there is a lag or delay in paying interest. Nevertheless, interest expense should be recorded for all days the money has been borrowed.

The accumulated amount of unpaid interest expense at the end of the accounting period is calculated and recorded in an accrued expenses payable type of account. In Exhibit 10.1, accrued interest payable at year-end is the second component of the accrued expenses payable liability. In our example, the amount of unpaid interest expense at year-end is fairly small, only $75,000. Generally speaking, accrued interest payable is not reported as a separate liability in external financial statements, although there is no rule against it.

Accounting Issues

First off, I have to tell you that the accrual of the liability for unpaid expenses depends on the good faith of the business in doing the calculations of these amounts—many of which involve arbitrary estimates and forecasts. This is one area that can be used for "massaging the numbers." This pejorative term refers to the deliberate manipulation of amounts recorded for sales revenue and expenses to record a higher (or lower) amount of profit for the period.

All I can do here is caution you that some businesses lay a heavy hand on the amounts recorded in their sales revenue and expense accounts, in order to smooth profit year to year or to give the profit for the year an artificial boost. Of course, these companies do not disclose in their financial statements that they have massaged their accounting numbers to nudge profit up (or down).

It would be proper to include in interest expense other types of borrowing costs, such as loan application and processing fees, so-called points charged by lenders, and other incidental costs of borrowing, such as legal fees and so on. Generally, however, most businesses put such extra charges in operating expense accounts. So, the interest expense in the income statement is just that—the interest on its debts for the period.

As I allude to earlier in the chapter, accrued interest payable usually is not reported as a separate liability in a company's year-end balance sheet. However, if this particular liability were large, it very well should be reported separately in the balance sheet. If a business is seriously behind in paying interest on its debts, the liability for unpaid interest should be prominently reported in its balance sheet, to call attention to this situation.

This last comment segues into the messy topic regarding how to present the financial statements of a business that is in serious financial trouble and is in default on its debt. One basic premise of financial statement accounting is called the *going concern assumption*. The accountant assumes that unless there is clear evidence to the contrary, the business will continue to operate in a normal manner and will not be forced into involuntary termination and liquidation of its assets. When a company is in serious default on its debt obligations, the creditors have the right to enforce their claims and in the extreme case shut the business down.

To stave off the drastic effects from unpaid creditors who may force it to shut down, the business can file for bankruptcy protection. This is a complicated area of law, beyond the scope of this book. If there is a serious threat of such legal actions by creditors against the business, the financial statements of the business should make full disclosure of its precarious financial situation.

EXHIBIT 11.1—INCOME TAX EXPENSE AND INCOME TAX PAYABLE

Dollar Amounts in Thousands

INCOME STATEMENT FOR YEAR

Sales Revenue	$ 52,000
Cost of Goods Sold Expense	(33,800)
Selling, General, and Adm. Expenses	(12,480)
Depreciation Expense	(785)
Interest Expense	(545)
Income Tax Expense	(1,748)
Net Income	$ 2,642

A relatively small amount of the income tax expense for the year is unpaid at year-end, which is recorded in the Income Tax Payable liability account.

BALANCE SHEET AT YEAR-END

ASSETS

Cash	$ 3,265
Accounts Receivable	5,000
Inventory	8,450
Prepaid Expenses	960
Property, Plant, and Equipment	16,500
Accumulated Depreciation	(4,250)
Intangible Assets	5,575
Total Assets	**$35,500**

LIABILITIES and STOCKHOLDERS' EQUITY

Accounts Payable	$ 3,320
Accrued Expenses Payable	1,515
Income Tax Payable	165
Short-Term Notes Payable	3,125
Long-Term Notes Payable	4,250
Capital Stock	8,125
Retained Earnings	15,000
Total Liabilities and Stockholders' Equity	**$35,500**

11

INCOME TAX EXPENSE AND ITS LIABILITY

Federal and State Income Taxation of Business Profit

Please refer to Exhibit 11.1 at the start of the chapter, which highlights the connection between *income tax expense* in the income statement and the *income tax payable* liability in the balance sheet. A small part of the company's total income tax expense for the year, which is based on its *taxable income* for the year, has not been paid at year-end. This remaining balance will be paid in the near future. The unpaid portion stays in the company's income tax payable liability account until paid.

The business in our example is *incorporated*; the business decided on this form of legal organization (instead of a partnership or limited liability company). A corporation, being a separate person in the eyes of the law, has several important advantages. However, profit-motivated business corporations have one serious disadvantage—they are subject to federal and state income tax on their profits, or, to be more accurate, they owe tax based on their *taxable income*, which is profit before income tax.

The business in this example is a regular, or so-called C corporation. Under the federal income tax law, small or S corporations, partnerships, and limited liability companies are "pass-through" tax entities—these entities pay no income tax themselves but instead serve as conduits. Their annual taxable income is transferred, or passed through, to their owners, who include their shares of the business's taxable income in their individual income tax returns for the year. In this way these entities

avoid the so-called double taxation of business profit—first in the hands of the business corporation, and second in the hands of its stockholders (to the extent that net income is distributed as cash dividends to them).

The first point to keep in mind is that a business corporation must earn *taxable income* to owe income tax. The simplest way to pay no income tax is to have no taxable income, or to have a loss for tax purposes. Of course a business wants to earn profit, but earning a profit comes with the burden of sharing its pretax profit with Uncle Sam and with the states that levy a tax on business profit earned within their borders.

A second point to keep in mind is that there are many loopholes and options in the federal income tax code—to say nothing about state income tax laws—that reduce or postpone income tax. I'm sure that you're aware of the complexity of the federal income tax law. That's an understatement, if I've ever heard one.

It takes thousands of pages of tax law to define taxable income. Most businesses use income tax professionals to help them determine their taxable income, and to advise them how to minimize the income taxes they must pay. In any one year, a business might take advantage of several different features of the tax code to minimize its taxable income for the year, or to shift taxable income to future years.

For the business example, I have to simplify. The business pays both federal and state income taxes based on its taxable income. Furthermore, I assume in the example that the accounting methods used to prepare its income statement are exactly the same methods used to determine its annual taxable income. In this example, the company's earnings before income tax are $4,390,000 (you can refer back to Exhibit 2.2 to check this). I assume that this amount is its taxable income for income tax.

The income tax expense amount is not all that simple to calculate, because of several factors. As you see in Exhibit 11.1, the income tax is $1,748,000, which is about 40% of taxable income. Keep in mind that the business pays both federal and state income taxes.

The federal income tax law requires that a business make installment payments during the year so that close to 100% of its annual income tax should be paid by the end of the tax year. Actually, a relatively small fraction of the total annual income tax may not be paid by year-end without any penalty (although this can get very complicated).

The company in this example paid most of its income taxes during the year. At year-end it still owes the federal and state tax authorities only $165,000 of its annual income tax. The unpaid portion is recorded in the *income tax payable* liability account, as you see in Exhibit 11.1.

The federal income tax law changes year to year; Congress is always tinkering with, or, shall we say, fine-tuning the tax code. Old loopholes are shut down; new loopholes open up. Tax rates have changed over time. For these reasons the fraction of annual income tax that is unpaid at year-end is hard to predict. However, if the year-end income tax liability is a large fraction of the income tax expense for the year, I'd advise you to take a closer look.

Accounting Issues

A business may opt to use certain accounting methods to determine its annual taxable income that are different from the accounting methods used to report sales revenue and expenses in its income statement. The objective is to postpone payment of income tax to later years. In this situation, financial reporting standards require that the amount of income tax expense in the income statement be consistent with the amount of earnings before income tax in the income statement. The idea is to report a normal amount of income tax expense, which is deducted from the earnings before income tax in the income statement.

However, the actual amount of income tax owed to the government on taxable income for the year can be very different than the normal income tax expense. Suppose a business reports $10,000,000 earnings before income tax in its income statement, and the normal income tax would be $3,500,000 on this amount of taxable income. However, the business uses different accounting methods for income tax, and its actual income tax owed for the year is only, say, $2,500,000.

Assume that this difference is only temporary and will eventually reverse itself such that in future years the business will owe more income tax than will be reported in its future income statements. The business records the full $3,500,000 amount of income tax, even though it owes only $2,500,000 for the year. The additional $1,000,000 needed to get the income tax expense up to the full $3,500,000 normal amount is recorded in a *deferred income tax liability* account—on the grounds that sooner or later the business will have to pay the additional $1,000,000 to the government.

I should tell you that there are many other problems in reporting income tax expense and income tax liabilities in business financial statements. These topics are very technical and beyond the scope of this book.

The footnotes to a company's financial statements should include a schedule reconciling the actual income tax owed for the year (based on taxable income for the year) with the normal income tax expense reported in the income statement. I regret to tell you that this is one of the most difficult footnotes you see in financial statements.

Accounting for income tax expense is a prime example of the *conditional* and *tentative* nature of financial statements. The numbers reported in financial statements would seem to be the final word on profit performance for the year and financial condition at the end of the year. Accountants do not have a crystal ball to see into the future, of course. Financial statements are provisional and subject to later revision.

The amount of income tax expense recorded for the year and the corresponding balance sheet account are subject to revision after the close of the year. The Internal Revenue Service (IRS) may have disagreements with the income tax returns filed by the business. Indeed, the IRS may do a full-scale audit and have many disagreements.

Some businesses push the envelope in interpreting the income tax law for determining annual taxable income. Or, a business may play it straight in how it reads the law. Even so, the income tax law is very complex and not clear-cut on many points. In short, there's always the possibility that the IRS may claim more income tax (or perhaps even make a refund).

EXHIBIT 12.1—NET INCOME AND RETAINED EARNINGS; EARNINGS PER SHARE (EPS)

Dollar Amounts in Thousands, Except Earnings per Share

BALANCE SHEET AT YEAR-END

ASSETS

Cash	$ 3,265
Accounts Receivable	5,000
Inventory	8,450
Prepaid Expenses	960
Property, Plant, and Equipment	16,500
Accumulated Depreciation	(4,250)
Intangible Assets	5,575
Total Assets	$35,500

INCOME STATEMENT FOR YEAR

Sales Revenue	$ 52,000
Cost of Goods Sold Expense	(33,800)
Selling, General, and Adm. Expenses	(12,480)
Depreciation Expense	(785)
Interest Expense	(545)
Income Tax Expense	(1,748)
Net Income	$ 2,642
Earnings per Share	$ 3.30

Bottom-line profit, or net income, increases the Retained Earnings owners' equity account. (This account is decreased by dividends paid to shareholders.)

LIABILITIES and STOCKHOLDERS' EQUITY

Accounts Payable	$ 3,320
Accrued Expenses Payable	1,515
Income Tax Payable	165
Short-Term Notes Payable	3,125
Long-Term Notes Payable	4,250
Capital Stock (800,000 shares)	8,125
Retained Earnings	15,000
Total Liabilities and Stockholders' Equity	$35,500

12

NET INCOME AND RETAINED EARNINGS; EARNINGS PER SHARE (EPS)

Net Income into Retained Earnings

Exhibit 12.1 at the start of the chapter highlights the connection from *net income* in the income statement to *retained earnings* in the balance sheet, and from net income to a new item that I show for the first time—*earnings per share* (EPS). This chapter explains that earning profit increases the retained earnings account. Also, I introduce earnings per share (EPS).

Suppose a business has $10 million total assets and $3 million total liabilities (including both non-interest-bearing operating liabilities and interest-bearing notes payable). Over the years, its owners have invested $4 million capital in the business. So, liabilities and owners' equity provide $7 million of the company's total assets. Now, where did the other $3 million of assets come from?

Assets don't just drop down like "manna from heaven." (My old accounting professor was the first person I heard use this phrase, and I've never forgotten it.) The other $3 million of assets must have come from profit the business earned but did not distribute—from *retained earnings*.

Two basic owners' equity accounts are needed—one for capital invested by the owners and one for retained earnings. When a business distributes money to its owners, it must distinguish between returning capital they have invested in the business (which is not taxable to them) versus dividing profit among them (which is taxable). A business corporation is required to keep separate accounts for capital stock and retained earnings.

The income statement reports that the business earned $2,642,000 bottom-line profit, or net income for the year (Exhibit 12.1). Net income is recorded as an increase in the retained earnings account, which is one of the two owners' equity accounts in the balance sheet (the other being capital stock). The retained earnings account is so named because annual profit is entered as an increase in the account, and distributions to owners from profit are entered as decreases in the account.

During the year, the business paid $750,000 cash dividends from net income to its stockholders. (You can check this out in Exhibit 3.1.) Therefore, its retained earnings increased only $1,892,000 during the year. At the end of the year, its retained earnings balance stands at $15,000,000, which is the cumulative result from all years the company has been in existence.

Notice in this example that the company has a relatively large retained earnings balance compared with its total assets and other balance sheet accounts. This signals that the business has been profitable in the past. However, we can't tell from the balance sheet whether the company suffered a loss one or more years in the past. By the way, if a company's losses over the years were larger than its profits, its retained earnings account would have a *negative* balance, which generally is called *accumulated deficit* or some similar title.

Many people, even some experienced business managers, are confused about retained earnings. They mistakenly think that retained earnings refers to an asset or, more specifically, is cash. No, a thousand times no! Retained earnings is not an asset and certainly is not cash. Yet, I can see that the name of this balance sheet account may mislead people into thinking that retained earnings refers to money that the business has squirreled away.

Instead of "retained earnings," the title "amount of total assets from earning profit kept in the business" might be clearer. This alternative title would remind the financial statement reader that making profit is one of the ways a business increases its assets. Suppose a business earns $1,000,000 profit. Basically, the amount of its total assets increases $1,000,000. To keep the books in balance, the accountant records a $1,000,000 increase in the retained earnings account.

In short, the balance in retained earnings explains one source of the total assets of a business. Other sources include money invested in the business by its owners (reported in capital stock) and money borrowed by the business (reported in notes payable accounts). Making profit and keeping it in the business added $15,000,000 to the total assets of the business (see Exhibit 12.1). You must look in the asset section of the balance sheet to see which particular assets the business owns.

When a business retains some (or all) of its annual net income, the retained profit should be considered as an addition to the ongoing capital base of the business. Businesses do not generally go back and pay a dividend from prior years' profits—although not too long ago Microsoft did just that because it had piled up a huge cash hoard and had no other investment uses for the money.

Looking down the road to the end of a business—after closing its doors, liquidating all of its assets, and paying off all of its liabilities, the business would distribute its remaining cash balance to its shareowners. The first layer of this final cash distribution to its shareowners is return of the capital they invested in the business. The remaining amount would be the final dividend (which is taxable).

Earnings per Share (EPS)

Net income, the bottom line in the income statement, is the profit measure for the business as a whole. Earnings per share (EPS) is the profit measure for each ownership unit, or each share of capital stock for a business corporation.

Suppose in our example that you own 16,000 shares, or exactly 2% of the 800,000 shares of capital stock issued by the business. Several years ago you purchased these shares by investing $120,000 in the business, when it was just starting up. You're one of the original stockholders. Your $120,000 capital investment divided by your 16,000 shares means that your cost is $7.50 per share. Later investors paid more per share.

We can tell this from the company's balance sheet (see Exhibit 12.1). The $8,125,000 balance in the company's capital stock account divided by the 800,000 capital stock shares outstanding works out to an average of more than $10 per share. So, the later investors must have paid more than $10 per share, perhaps $20 or more per share.

Since you own only 2% of the total capital stock shares outstanding, you are a passive, outside investor in the business. You do not participate actively in managing the company. Of course you're entitled to 2% of any cash dividends paid from profit, and you control 2% of the votes on matters that have to be put to a vote of stockholders.

As a stockholder you are provided a copy of the company's annual (and quarterly) financial reports. Needless to say, you're very interested in the company's profit performance. You could take the view that 2% of annual net income belongs to you, which is a $52,840 slice of the company's $2,642,000 net income. This is your cut of the net income pie. Or you could look at earnings per share (EPS), which is net income divided by the average number of capital stock shares outstanding during the year. In this example, EPS for the year just ended works out to $3.30 per share.

Earnings per share (EPS) is a very important investment number for *public* companies whose shares are traded on the New York Stock Exchange or through another national stock market such as Nasdaq. Public companies must report EPS at the bottom of their income statements. Nonpublic companies can report EPS if they want to, though I don't think many do. I discuss EPS further in Chapter 17.

Here, I just mention that EPS plays the key role in putting a market value on a share of stock in a business. For example, suppose I offer to buy 1,000 of your shares. You might offer to sell them at 15 times the $3.30 EPS, or $49.50 per share. Of course, I might not be willing to pay this price. In any case, it's a very important point of reference. Earnings per share of public companies get a lot of attention in the press.

Accounting Issues

The retained earnings balance is what's left after adding net income earned by the business and deducting dividends paid from net income to the shareowners. Accounting problems don't concern retained earnings but rather sales revenue and expenses, which I've explained over the last several chapters. If net income is incorrect, then the retained earnings amount is incorrect.

There are some technical aspects of retained earnings, which are beyond the scope of this book. By and large, the financial reporting of retained earnings is very straightforward and non-controversial. But reporting EPS is another matter altogether.

There are several problems in calculating EPS. Many companies have to report not just one, but two measures for EPS—one based on the actual number of stock shares outstanding (in the hands of shareowners) and a second EPS that includes additional shares that the business is potentially committed to issue in the future. I discuss EPS further in Chapter 17.

EXHIBIT 13.1—CASH FLOW FROM OPERATING (PROFIT-MAKING) ACTIVITIES

Dollar Amounts in Thousands

BALANCE SHEET	Start of Year	End of Year	Change	STATEMENT OF CASH FLOWS FOR YEAR		
Assets				Net Income—See Income Statement	$ 2,642	
Cash	$ 3,735	$ 3,265	$ (470)	Accounts Receivable Increase	(320)	
Accounts Receivable	4,680	5,000	320	Inventory Increase	(935)	
Inventory	7,515	8,450	935	Prepaid Expenses Increase	(275)	
Prepaid Expenses	685	960	275	Depreciation Expense	785	
Property, Plant, and Equipment	13,450	16,500	3,050	Accounts Payable Increase	645	
Accumulated Depreciation	(3,465)	(4,250)	(785)	Accrued Expenses Payable Increase	480	
Intangible Assets	5,000	5,575	575	Income Tax Payable Increase	83	
Total Assets	**$31,600**	**$35,500**		**Cash Flow from Operating Activities**		**$ 3,105**
Liabilities and Stockholders' Equity				Investments in Property, Plant, and Equipment	$(3,050)	
Accounts Payable	$ 2,675	$ 3,320	645	Investments in Intangible Assets	(575)	
Accrued Expenses Payable	1,035	1,515	480	**Cash Flow from Investing Activities**		**(3,625)**
Income Tax Payable	82	165	83			
Short-Term Notes Payable	3,000	3,125	125	Increase in Short-Term Notes Payable	$ 125	
Long-Term Notes Payable	3,750	4,250	500	Increase in Long-Term Notes Payable	500	
Capital Stock	7,950	8,125	175	Issue of Additional Capital Stock Shares	175	
Retained Earnings	13,108	15,000	1,892	Cash Dividends Paid Shareholders	(750)	
Total Liabilities and Stockholders' Equity	**$31,600**	**$35,500**		**Cash Flow from Financing Activities**		**50**
				Decrease in Cash during Year		**$ (470)**

13

CASH FLOW FROM OPERATING (PROFIT-MAKING) ACTIVITIES

Profit and Cash Flow from Profit: Not Identical Twins!

At this point we shift gears. Chapters 4 through 12 (except for Chapter 6) walk down the income statement. Each chapter explains how sales revenue or an expense is connected with its corresponding asset or liability. In short, sales revenue and expenses cause changes in assets and liabilities. You can't understand the balance sheet well without understanding how sales revenue and expenses drive many of the assets and liabilities in the balance sheet.

This chapter is the first of two that explain the *statement of cash flows*, which is the third primary financial statement reported by businesses in addition to the income statement and balance sheet. Exhibit 13.1 at the start of the chapter presents the cash flows statement of the business we have discussed since Chapter 1. Please take a moment to read down this statement. I'll make you a wager here. I bet you understand the second and third sections of the statement (*investing* activities and *financing* activities) much better than the first section (*operating* activities).

Exhibit 13.1 shows the balance sheets of the company at the start and end of the year and includes a column for changes in assets, liabilities, and stockholders' equity. This chapter focuses on the first section of the cash flows statement, which presents cash flows from the company's operating activities (i.e., its *profit-making* activities) during the year. As I'm sure you recall, a company's profit-making activities are reported in its income statement.

The main question on everyone's mind seems to be why profit doesn't equal cash flow. In this example, the company earned $2,642,000 net income over the year just ended. Why didn't earning this amount of profit generate the same amount of cash flow? The first section in the cash flows statement provides the answer to this question.

The last line in the first section is labeled "Cash Flow from Operating Activities" (see Exhibit 13.1). Frankly, this is not the best name in the world. I prefer to call it *cash flow from profit*. The term "operating activities" is accounting jargon for sales revenue and expenses, which are the profit-making activities or operations of a business. Much of the time I'll refer to this line as cash flow from profit, which is shorter and more descriptive, I think. In any case, from the cash flows statement we see that the company generated $3,105,000 cash flow from profit compared with its smaller $2,642,000 net income for the year.

Business managers have a double duty—first to earn profit, and second to convert the profit into cash as soon as possible. Waiting too long to turn profit into cash reduces its value because of the time value of money. Business managers should be clear on the difference between profit reported in the income statement and the amount of cash flow from profit during the year. Creditors and investors also should keep an eye on cash flow from profit (operating activities) and management's ability to control this very important number.

To get from net income to the cash flow result from net income, we have to make adjustments along the way. Each is caused by a change during the year in one of the company's operating assets and liabilities (i.e., the assets and liabilities directly involved in sales revenue and expenses). We shall look at these adjustments in the order shown in the company's statement of cash flows (data is from Exhibit 13.1 at the start of the chapter).

Changes in Assets and Liabilities That Drive Cash Flow from Operating Activities

1. **Accounts Receivable:** At year-end the company had $5,000,000 uncollected sales revenue, which is the ending balance of its accounts receivable. The $5,000,000 is included in sales revenue for determining profit. But the company did not receive this amount of cash from customers. The $5,000,000 is still in accounts receivable instead of cash at year-end. However, the company collected its $4,680,000 beginning balance of accounts receivable. The $4,680,000 collected minus $5,000,000 not collected results in a $320,000 negative impact on cash flow. See the first adjustment in the cash flow statement (Exhibit 13.1). If short, an increase in accounts receivable hurts cash flow from profit.

2. **Inventory:** Notice the rather large increase in the company's inventory during the year. This may or may not have been a smart business decision. Perhaps the business needed a larger inventory to meet higher sales demand, or maybe not. In any case, the $935,000 inventory increase has a negative impact on cash flow. The quickest way to explain this is as follows. Inventory is an investment in products in the process of being manufactured and finished products being held for sale. Increasing an investment means putting more money in the investment. See the second adjustment in the cash flow statement. In short, an increase in inventory hurts cash flow from operating activities (the profit-making activities of the business).

3. **Prepaid Expenses:** During the year, the company paid $960,000 for certain operating costs that will benefit next year, and therefore were not charged to expenses in the year. See the ending balance in the company's prepaid expenses account. The company paid $960,000 on top of its operating expenses for the year. But the company had $685,000 of prepaid expenses at the start of the year; these costs were paid last year and then charged to operating expenses in the year just ended. Taking into account both the beginning and ending balances in prepaid expenses, the company experiences only $275,000 drain on cash during the year. The $685,000 not paid minus $960,000 paid has a $275,000 negative impact on cash flow. See the third adjustment in the cash flow statement (Exhibit 13.1).

4. **Depreciation:** During the year the company recorded $785,000 depreciation expense, not by writing a check for this amount but by writing down the cost of its property, plant, and equipment. This write-down is recorded as an increase in the accumulated depreciation account, which is the contra or offset account deducted from the property, plant, and equipment asset account. These long-term operating assets are partially written down each year to record the wear and tear on them during every year of use. The company paid cash for the assets when it bought these

long-term resources. The company does not have to pay for them a second time when it uses them. In short, depreciation expense is not a cash outlay in the year recorded and therefore is a positive adjustment, or so-called add back for determining cash flow from profit. See the fourth adjustment in the cash flow statement.

The depreciation add back to net income can be explained another way. For the sake of argument here, assume all sales revenue had been collected in cash during the year. Part of this cash inflow from customers pays the company for the use of its long-term operating assets during the year. In a sense, the business "sells" a fraction of its fixed assets to its customers each year. In setting its sales prices, a business includes depreciation as a cost of doing business. So, each year a business recovers part of the capital invested in its fixed assets in cash flow from sales revenue. In short, the company in this example recaptured $785,000 of the investment in its property, plant, and equipment assets, which is a significant source of cash flow.

5. **Accounts Payable:** The ending balance in the company's accounts payable liability reveals that manufacturing costs and operating expenses were not fully paid during the year. The ending balance in this liability relieved the company of making cash payments in the amount of $3,320,000 (again see Exhibit 13.1). Not paying these costs avoids cash outflow, of course. Consider the other side of the coin, as well. The company started the year with $2,675,000 accounts payable. These liabilities were paid during the year. The $3,320,000 not paid minus $2,675,000 paid has a net $645,000 positive impact on cash flow. See the fifth adjustment in the cash flow statement.

6. **Accrued Expenses Payable:** This liability works virtually the same way as accounts payable. The company did not pay $1,515,000 of its expenses during the year, which is the balance in this liability at the end of the year. But the company did pay the $1,035,000 beginning amount of this liability. The $1,515,000 not paid minus $1,035,000 paid has a net $480,000 positive impact on cash flow. See the sixth adjustment in the cash flow statement.

7. **Income Tax Payable:** At the start of the year, the business owed the tax authorities $82,000 on taxable income from the previous year. This amount was paid early in the year. At the end of the year, the business owed $165,000 of its income tax expense for the year; this amount was not paid. The net effect is that the company paid $83,000 less to the government than its income tax expense for the year. See the positive adjustment for the increase in income tax payable in the cash flow statement.

Summing up the seven cash flow adjustments to net income:

• Increases in operating assets cause decreases in cash flow from profit; and decreases in operating assets result in increases in cash flow from profit.

• Increases in operating liabilities help cash flow from profit; and decreases in operating liabilities result in decreases in cash flow from profit.

See in Exhibit 13.1 that the combined net effect of the seven adjustments is that cash flow from profit is $3,105,000, which is $463,000 more than profit for the year. This difference between cash flow and bottom-line profit is due to the changes in the

EXHIBIT 13.2—DIRECT METHOD FORMAT FOR REPORTING CASH FLOW FROM OPERATING ACTIVITIES IN THE STATEMENT OF CASH FLOWS

Dollar Amounts in Thousands

Sales Revenue	$ 51,680
Cost of Goods Sold Expense	(34,760)
Operating Expenses	(11,630)
Interest Expense	(520)
Income Tax Expense	(1,665)
Cash Flow from Operating Activities	$ 3,105

company's operating assets and liabilities. In summary, the business realized $3,105,000 cash flow from its operating activities during the year. This source of cash flow is vital to every business.

The accounting profession's rule-making body in the United States, the Financial Accounting Standards Board (FASB), has expressed a preference regarding the reporting of cash flow from operating activities. You might be surprised that the format you see in the first section of Exhibit 13.1 is *not* the preferred method. What you see in Exhibit 13.1 is called the *indirect method* that uses changes in operating assets and liabilities to adjust net income, which leads down to cash flow from operating activities. Instead, the FASB prefers the *direct method* for this section of the statement of cash flows.

Exhibit 13.2 shows the *direct method* format for reporting cash flow from operating activities. The cash flow amounts from sales revenue and for expenses are presented "directly" in this format. The direct method format is supplemented with a schedule that summarizes the changes in operating assets and liabilities, pretty much the same way as the changes are presented by the indirect method shown in Exhibit 13.1.

Both formats report the same cash flow from operating activities, of course. Although the FASB expresses a clear preference for the direct method, the large majority of businesses decide on the indirect method in their external financial reports (which the FASB permits). Because of its popularity, I use the indirect method for the statement of cash flows in our business example.

An Alternative View of Cash Flow

You frequently see "cash flow" mentioned in the business and financial press. In reading these news items and articles, I'm not always certain what the reporter means by the term "cash flow." Reporters usually don't offer definitions of the term. When they do define cash flow, they don't necessarily mean the amount in the statement of cash flows called cash flow from operating activities. They often use some other measure of cash flow. So, be careful when reading an article that refers to cash flow.

One alternative definition of cash flow has become popular: earnings before interest, (income) tax, depreciation, and amortization (EBITDA). For our business example, EBITDA is determined as follows (dollar amounts in thousands):

Calculation of EBITDA

Net income	$2,642
+ Interest	545
+ Income tax	1,748
+ Depreciation	785
= EBITDA	$5,720

In my view, EBITDA is a rather odd and misleading way to look at cash flow from operating activities. EBITDA should be used carefully and with a crystal-clear understanding that this cash flow measure is not the bottom-line cash flow from operating activities, because cash flows for interest and income tax expenses are not taken into account, and because other factors affecting cash flow are ignored as well.

Keep in mind that changes in accounts receivable, inventory, prepaid expenses, accounts payable, accrued expenses payable, and income tax payable are ignored by the EBITDA definition of cash flow. If all these changes in operating assets and liabilities are relatively minor, then simply adding back depreciation (and amortization, if any) to net income might be acceptable. But typically these changes are significant and cannot be ignored.

A Final Warning: In some situations cash flow is pushed to the forefront and profit is pushed to the background. When a business's profit performance is lackluster or when a business reports a loss, the CEO may prefer to shift attention to cash flow (assuming cash flow is healthy). However, cash flow is not a substitute for profit. The oldest trick in the book is to divert attention from bad news to whatever good news you can find. Simply put, profit generates cash flow; cash flow does not generate profit.

Accounting Issues

Most financial statement readers have a good intuitive understanding of a balance sheet (assets, liabilities, and shareholders' equity), and they have a good intuitive understanding that profit equals sales revenue minus expenses. In contrast, most financial statement readers seem confused about cash flow from profit. They think that making profit means making money, and that cash increases the same amount as bottom-line profit. This is not true, however. Profit and cash flow are two different numbers, both of which are important in their own right.

In preparing financial statements for a business, the accountant should realize that the audience of the financial report probably is laboring under a misperception regarding cash flow. Ideally, the accountant should make an effort to clarify that profit is measured using *accrual-basis accounting*, in which several assets and liabilities are used to record sales and expenses. Readers should be reminded that cash flows of sales and expenses take place on different timetables, causing cash flow from profit to be a different amount from profit for the period.

However, accountants make no special efforts in explaining cash flow to financial statement readers. They assume that the readers have the same level of understanding of the statement of cash flows as they may have of the balance sheet and income statement. In my view, businesses and their accountants should do a much better job reporting cash flows. I have read countless statements of cash flows. Many are so complicated that you have to wonder whether the complications are deliberate. It's not unusual to find a cash flows statement of a public company that reports 30, 40, or more lines of technical information. And it is virtually impossible to reconcile all the items reported in the statement of cash flows with their corresponding assets and liabilities in the balance sheet.

I believe businesses should provide a more readable statement of cash flows. Furthermore, top management should provide a brief summary and discussion of the company's cash flows for the year. Instead, the large majority of businesses report a statement of cash flows that is very difficult and time-consuming to read, and they offer little or no comment regarding cash flows.

Frankly (as if I haven't been so far), I have a suspicion that some companies operate on the thin edge of cash flows—they barely keep cash flows under control. They don't want to talk about their cash flow problems in their financial reports. Managing cash flows is no easy task, especially when a business is only a day or a week away from a zero cash balance.

EXHIBIT 14.1—CASH FLOWS FROM INVESTING AND FINANCING ACTIVITIES
Dollar Amounts in Thousands

BALANCE SHEET	Start of Year	End of Year	Change		STATEMENT OF CASH FLOWS FOR YEAR		
Assets					Net Income—See Income Statement	$ 2,642	
Cash	$ 3,735	$ 3,265	$ (470)		Accounts Receivable Increase	(320)	
Accounts Receivable	4,680	5,000	320		Inventory Increase	(935)	
Inventory	7,515	8,450	935		Prepaid Expenses Increase	(275)	
Prepaid Expenses	685	960	275		Depreciation Expense	785	
Property, Plant, and Equipment	13,450	16,500	3,050		Accounts Payable Increase	645	
Accumulated Depreciation	(3,465)	(4,250)	(785)		Accrued Expenses Payable Increase	480	
Intangible Assets	5,000	5,575	575		Income Tax Payable Increase	83	
Total Assets	$31,600	$35,500			**Cash Flow from Operating Activities**		$ 3,105
Liabilities and Stockholders' Equity					Investments in Property, Plant, and Equipment	$(3,050)	
Accounts Payable	$ 2,675	$ 3,320	645		Investments in Intangible Assets	(575)	
Accrued Expenses Payable	1,035	1,515	480		**Cash Flow from Investing Activities**		(3,625)
Income Tax Payable	82	165	83				
Short-Term Notes Payable	3,000	3,125	125 ←	Increase in Short-Term Notes Payable	$ 125	
Long-Term Notes Payable	3,750	4,250	500 ←	Increase in Long-Term Notes Payable	500	
Capital Stock	7,950	8,125	175 ←	Issue of Additional Capital Stock Shares	175	
Retained Earnings	13,108	15,000	1,892 ←	Cash Dividends Paid Shareholders	(750)	
Total Liabilities and Stockholders' Equity	$31,600	$35,500			**Cash Flow from Financing Activities**		50
					Decrease in Cash during Year		$ (470)

14

CASH FLOWS FROM INVESTING AND FINANCING ACTIVITIES

Rounding Out the Statement of Cash Flows

Please refer to Exhibit 14.1 at the start of the chapter. The preceding chapter explains the first of the three sections in the statement of cash flows, which without doubt is the hardest of the three to understand. This chapter explains the other two sections of the cash flows statement, which are a piece of cake to understand compared with the first section that reports cash flow from operating activities.

The second section of the statement of cash flows (see Exhibit 14.1) summarizes the *investments* made by the business during the year in long-term operating assets. In the example, the business spent $3,050,000 for new fixed assets (tangible long-term operating assets). See the line extending from this expenditure in the statement of cash flows to the property, plant, and equipment asset account in the balance sheet. In addition, the business increased its investment in intangible assets $575,000 during the year.

The investing activities section of the cash flows statement also includes proceeds from disposals of investments (net of tax), if there are any such disposals. In our example, the business did not dispose of any of its long-term operating assets during the year—tangible or intangible. I should mention in passing that an ongoing business normally makes some disposals of fixed assets during the year.

The third section of the statement of cash flows (see Exhibit 14.1 again) reports the cash flows of what are called *financing activities*. The term "financing" refers to dealings between the business and its sources of capital (i.e., its debtholders and its stockholders). The business in our example increased its short-term and long-term debt during the year. It also raised $175,000 from issuing new capital stock shares. See the lines of connection from the lines in the statement of cash flows to the corresponding balance sheet accounts in Exhibit 14.1.

The business distributed $750,000 cash dividends to its shareowners during the year. Cash dividends are included in the financing activities section of the cash flows statement. Why not put cash dividends from profit next to cash flow from profit (i.e., operating activities)? I say more about the placement of cash dividends later in the chapter. Its $2,642,000 of net income for the year increases the company's retained earnings account, and the $750,000 of cash dividends decreases the shareholders' equity account. So the net increase in retained earnings is $1,892,000 (see Exhibit 14.1).

The bottom line of the statement of cash flows is the $470,000 decrease in cash during the year (see Exhibit 14.1). Well, perhaps I shouldn't call the change in cash the bottom line. The accounting authorities would not be amused. The term "bottom line" is more or less reserved for the last line of the income statement. But I see nothing wrong with referring to the bottom line of the cash flows statement. That line is the final, net result of all three types of activities that determine the increase or decrease in cash during the year.

Seeing the Big Picture of Cash Sources and Uses

Earning profit is a vital source of cash inflow to every business. Profit can be viewed as the *internal* source of cash flow—money generated by the business itself without going outside the company to external sources of capital. Chapter 13 explains that the company generated $3,105,000 cash flow during the year just ended from its profit-making (operating) activities. Profit provided more than three million dollars of money for the business, and this isn't chicken feed.

The obvious question is: What did the business do with its cash flow from profit? The remainder of the cash flows statement answers this important question. The rest of the cash flows statement reports other sources of cash that were tapped by the business during the year that provided additional capital to the business. And, most important, the statement of cash flows reveals what the business did with all this money.

From its profit-making activities the company generated $3,105,000 cash during the year. What *could* it do with this money? (We'll look at what it actually did in just a moment.) One option is simply to increase its cash balance—just let the money pile up in the company's checking account. This is not a very productive use of the cash, unless the business is on the ragged edge and desperately needs to increase its day-to-day working cash balance. The business could also pay down some of its liabilities. Or the company could use some of the money to pay cash dividends to its stockholders.

In fact, the business did pay $750,000 cash dividends to its stockholders during the year. The amount of cash dividends to shareholders is one of the key items reported in the statement of cash flows—see the third section of the cash flows statement in Exhibit 14.1. After subtracting $750,000 cash dividends from the $3,105,000 cash flow from profit, the company had $2,355,000 cash flow remaining from operating activities. You may ask: What did the business do with this cash?

To modernize and expand its production and sales capacity, during the year the business invested $3,625,000 in new long-term operating assets (refer to Exhibit 14.1 again). These cash outlays are called *capital expenditures*, to emphasize the long-term nature of investing capital in these assets. You may have noticed that the total amount of capital expenditures was considerably more than the amount of cash flow from profit net of cash dividends ($3,625,000 capital expenditures less $2,355,000 cash flow from profit net of cash dividends = $1,270,000 shortfall). This money had to come from somewhere.

A business has three sources to cover such a cash shortfall: (1) borrow more money on short-term and long-term debt; (2) secure additional capital from shareowners by issuing new capital stock shares; and (3) spend down its cash balance. The business in our example did some of all three, as seen in the following summary (amounts from Exhibit 14.1):

***Sources Used to Cover Amount Spent on Capital
Expenditures during Year in Excess of Cash Flow
from Operating Activities Net of Cash Dividends***

Short-term debt increase	$ 125,000
Long-term debt increase	500,000
Issue of new capital stock shares	175,000
Decrease in cash balance	470,000
Total	$1,270,000

When a business is growing year to year, its cash flow from profit net of cash dividends usually does not provide all the cash it needs for its capital expenditures. Therefore, the business has to expand its debt and equity capital, which the business did in our example. Chapter 16 examines the impact of business growth and decline on cash flow from operating activities.

Business managers, lenders, and investors keep a close watch on capital expenditures. These cash outlays are a bet on the future by the company. The business is saying, in effect, that it needs the new fixed assets to maintain or improve its competitive position, or to expand its facilities for future growth. These are some of the most critical decisions business managers make.

Making capital investments is always risky. On one hand, who knows what will happen in the future? On the other hand, not making such investments may sign the death warrant of a business. By not making such investments, the company may fall behind its competition and lose market share that would be impossible to regain. Then again, being overinvested and having excess capacity can be an albatross around the neck of a business.

In any case, the business laid out $3,625,000 during the year for new assets (see Exhibit 14.1 again). In doing so, the business had to make key financing decisions—where to get the money for the asset purchases. As already mentioned, the business decided it could allow its working cash balance to drop $470,000. The company's ending cash balance is $3,265,000, which relative to its $52,000,000 annual sales revenue equals about three weeks of sales revenue.

I should point out that there are no general standards or guidelines regarding how large a company's working cash balance should be. Most business managers would view the company's cash balance in this example as adequate, I think. Just how much cash cushion does a business need as a safety reserve to protect against unfavorable developments?

What if the economy takes a nosedive, or what if the company has a serious falloff in sales? What if some of its accounts receivable are not collected on time? What if the company is not able to sell its inventory soon enough to keep the cash flow cycle in motion? What if it doesn't have enough money to pay its employees on time? There are no easy answers to these cash dilemmas.

The business could have forgone cash dividends in order to keep its working cash balance at a higher level. In all likelihood, its stockholders want a cash dividend on their investments in the business, and the board of directors was under pressure to deliver cash dividends. In any case, the business distributed $750,000 cash dividends, which are reported in the financing activities section in the cash flows statement (Exhibit 14.1).

In summary, the cash flows statement deserves as much attention and scrutiny as the income statement and balance sheet. Though not too likely, a company making a profit could be headed for liquidity problems (having too little ready cash) or solvency problems (not being able to pay liabilities on time). Profit does not guarantee liquidity and solvency. The cash flows statement should be read carefully to see if there are any danger signs or red flags.

At the end of Chapter 13 I mention that the cash flows statements reported by most public corporations are cluttered with a lot of detail—often far too much detail, in my opinion. One could get the impression that companies are deliberately making their cash flow statements hard to read, though this view may be too cynical.

My advice is to focus mainly on the big-ticket items and skip the smaller details in reading a statement of cash flows. Stand back and try to see the big picture. The income statements reported by most public corporations have far fewer lines of information compared with cash flows statements and are generally much easier to understand. This is an odd state of affairs indeed.

Accounting Issues

You might suppose that cash flows are a straightforward matter. But in fact there are many technical accounting problems in reporting cash flows. For example, should the cash flows connected with the discontinued operations of a business be reported separately from its ongoing, recurring cash flows? Should cash flows of certain short-term activities be reported gross or net? These cash flow issues are beyond the scope of this book. (I can almost hear you breathing easier here.)

One thing comes across loud and clear in the authoritative pronouncement on reporting cash flows from the Financial Accounting Standards Board (FASB). A business should not include cash flow per share in its financial reports. In particular, a business should not report cash flow from operating activities per share. You might recall that public companies are required to report earnings (net income) per share (EPS). The FASB does not want financial statement readers to confuse EPS with cash flow.

One of my criticisms of the statement of cash flows—aside from the huge number of lines reported by most companies in this financial statement—is the placement of cash dividends in the financing activities section of the statement. Instead, I favor placing cash dividends immediately under cash flow from operating activities. Deducting the amount of cash dividends from cash flow from operating activities would highlight the amount of cash flow the company had available for general business purposes.

To illustrate this alternative treatment of cash dividends in the statement of cash flows for our business example (in thousands of dollars from Exhibit 14.1):

Cash flow from operating activities	$3,105
Cash dividends	(750)
Cash flow available for general purposes	$2,355

The purpose is to show more clearly how much of the cash flow from profit was available to the business after cash dividends. The financial statement reader could conveniently compare cash flow from profit and cash dividends to share owners. The financial statement reader could easily size up dividends against the amount of cash flow from profit, and see the amount of cash remaining for other needs of the business.

The Financial Accounting Standards Board (FASB) never asked me for advice on this matter. The FASB decided that dividends should be reported in the financing activities section of the cash flows statement. My view is that businesses should have more options regarding where to place cash dividends in the statement of cash flows.

Exhibit 15.1—THREE FINANCIAL STATEMENTS AND FOOTNOTES

15

FOOTNOTES TO
FINANCIAL STATEMENTS

Financial Statements—Brief Review

Exhibit 15.1 at the start of the chapter shows the principal components of the three financial statements of a business and shows that *footnotes* are included with the three statements. Footnotes are the fourth essential part of every financial report—the three financial statements plus their footnotes. This chapter explains the reasons for and problems with footnotes.

Before discussing footnotes, it's a good idea at this point to review the three financial statements of a business that I explain in previous chapters.

1. ***Balance Sheet:*** Also called the statement of financial condition, the balance sheet is a summary of the company's assets, liabilities, and owners' (stockholders') equity at the close of business on the last day of the income statement period. To understand a balance sheet, you need to understand the differences between the basic types of assets (inventory versus property, plant, and equipment, for instance), and the differences between operating liabilities (mainly accounts payable and accrued expenses payable) versus debt on which the business pays interest. Also, you should know the difference between the two different sources of owners' equity—capital invested by the owners in the business versus profit earned but not distributed to owners, which is called *retained earnings*.

2. ***Income Statement:*** This is the summary of a company's sales revenue and expenses for the period (the profit-making activities of the business) and, of course, it reports the company's bottom-line profit or net income for the period. A publicly owned business corporation must report earnings per share (EPS) with its income statement. A nonpublic company doesn't have to report earnings per share.

3. ***Statement of Cash Flows:*** Making a profit has cash flow effects, that's for sure! But the amount of cash flow from making profit during the year does not equal net income for the year. This financial statement divides cash flows into three groups. The first section provides a trail from net income to cash flow from *operating (profit-making) activities*. The second section summarizes the cash flow of the company's *investing activities* during the year. The third section summarizes the cash flow from the company's *financing activities* during the year. The cash flows statement exposes the financial strategy of the business. You have to interpret this statement very carefully to get a good sense of its financial strategy.

In short, the three financial statements report on the three financial imperatives facing every business—to make a profit, to remain in healthy financial condition, and to make good use of cash flow.

Although authoritative financial reporting standards in the United States, called *generally accepted accounting principles* (GAAP) do not strictly require it, most businesses—large and small, public and private—present two-year or three-year financial statements. This multiyear presentation allows financial statement readers to make comparisons between the year just ended and the preceding year, and the year before that. The federal agency that regulates financial reporting by public corporations, the Securities and Exchange Commission (SEC), requires three-year comparative financial statements.

According to various estimates, there are about 10,000 *public* companies in the United States. The financial reports of public companies are required to be audited by an independent certified public accountant (CPA) firm. The largest four international CPA firms (called the Big Four) audit the large majority of public companies. There are millions of *private* businesses in the United States. Private companies may or may not decide to have their financial reports audited by an independent CPA firm. Generally, they are not legally required to have audits. I discuss financial report audits in Chapter 21.

Why Footnotes?

Without footnotes, financial statements would be incomplete, and possibly misleading. Footnotes are an essential *supplement* to financial statements. Each financial statement is presented on one page, or at most two pages, in a financial report. Each financial statement is very condensed and presents highly compacted information.

It comes down to this: The lenders and investors in a business need more information than can be put into the financial statements. I suppose you could integrate this additional information into each financial statement. But can you imagine reading a balance sheet or an income statement that runs 5, 10, or 20 pages long? I don't think so. Therefore, the practical solution is to present the additional information in the form of supplementary footnotes to the financial statements.

Top-level managers should not forget that they are responsible for the company's financial statements *and the accompanying footnotes*. The footnotes are an integral, inseparable part of a financial report. Financial statements state this fact on the bottom of each page, usually worded as follows:

The accompanying footnotes to the financial statements are an integral part of these statements.

The CPA auditor's report covers footnotes as well as the financial statements.

In short, footnotes are necessary because the additional information provided in the footnotes is needed by financial statement readers. The overarching premise of financial reporting is *adequate disclosure*, so that all those who have a legitimate interest in the financial affairs of the business are provided the relevant information they need to make informed decisions and to protect their interests in the business.

Ideally, footnotes should be written in an understandable manner, and every effort should be made to use language and visual layouts and exhibits that are clear and reasonably easy to follow. In other words, financial reports should be *transparent*. The lack of transparency in financial reports has come in for much criticism, especially regarding footnotes that are so dense and obtuse that even a lawyer would have trouble reading them. More on this point later in the chapter.

Two Types of Footnotes

One type of footnote identifies and discusses the key accounting methods used by the business. For several expenses, and even for sales revenue, a business can choose between two (or more) acceptable accounting methods. The company's selections of accounting methods should be made clear in its footnotes. A footnote is needed for each significant accounting choice by the business.

For instance, the particular accounting method used to determine the company's cost of goods sold expense and ending inventory cost should be identified. The following footnote is from a recent financial report of Caterpillar Inc. (page A-11 of Caterpillar's 2007 10-K form filed with the Securities and Exchange Commission). *Warning:* Footnotes assume that you are familiar with accounting terminology.

Inventories are stated at the lower of cost or market. Cost is principally determined using the last-in, first-out (LIFO) method. The value of inventories on the LIFO basis represented about 75% of total inventories at December 31, 2007 and 2006, and about 80% of total inventories at December 31, 2005.

If the FIFO (first-in, first-out) method had been in use, inventories would have been $2,617 million, $2,403 million, and $2,345 million higher than reported at December 31, 2007, 2006, and 2005, respectively.

By the way, you might notice that in its financial statements Caterpillar reports dollar amounts in millions.

This footnote reveals that Caterpillar's inventories at these year-ends would have been more than $2 billion higher if the company had selected an alternative accounting method. And its cost of goods sold expense for each year would have been different.

Companies disclose their depreciation and amortization methods in footnotes. For example, Caterpillar's footnote from its 2007 10-K reads:

Depreciation of plant and equipment is computed principally using accelerated methods. Depreciation on equipment leased to others, primarily for Financial Products, is computed using the straight-line method over the term of the lease. The depreciable basis is the original cost of the equipment less the estimated residual value of the equipment at the end of the lease term. In 2007, 2006, and 2005 Cat Financial depreciation on equipment leased to others was $671 million, $631 million, and $615 million respectively, and was included in "Other operating expenses" in Statement 1. In 2007, 2006, and 2005 consolidated depreciation expense was $1,725 million, $1,554 million, and $1,444 million respectively. Amortization of purchased intangibles is computed principally using the straight-line method, generally not to exceed a period of 20 years.

By the way, companies are no longer required to systematically write off (amortize) the cost of their intangible assets, which I discuss in Chapter 9.

Other common footnotes explain the consolidation of the company's financial statements. Most large businesses consist of a family of corporations under the control of one parent company. The financial statements of each corporation are grouped together into one integrated set of financial statements. Intercorporate dealings are eliminated as if there were only one entity. Affiliated companies in which the business has made investments are not consolidated if the company does not have a controlling interest in the other business.

In addition to footnotes that identify accounting methods, many footnotes are needed to provide important information that cannot be placed in the financial statements themselves. For example, the maturity dates, interest rates, collateral or other security provisions, and other details of the long-term debt of a business are presented in footnotes. Annual rentals required under long-term operating leases are given. Details regarding stock options and employee stock ownership plans are spelled out, and the dilution effects on earnings per share are illustrated in footnotes.

Major lawsuits and other legal actions against the company are discussed in footnotes. Details about the company's employees' retirement and pension plans are disclosed in footnotes. Obligations of the business to pay for postretirement health and medical costs of retired employees are presented in footnotes.

The list of possible footnotes is a long one. In preparing its annual report, a business needs to go down an exhaustive checklist of items that may have to be disclosed, and then actually write the footnotes. This is no easy task. The business has to explain in a relatively small space what can be rather complex.

Management Discretion in Writing Footnotes

Managers have to rely on the experts—the chief financial officer of the organization, legal counsel, and the outside CPA auditor—to go through the checklist of footnotes that may be required. Once every required footnote has been identified, key decisions still have to be made regarding each footnote. Managers have a good deal of discretion and latitude regarding just how candid to be and how much detail to reveal in each footnote.

Clearly, managers should not give away the farm—they should not divulge information that would damage a competitive advantage that the business enjoys. Managers don't have to help their competitors. The idea is to help the company's debtholders and stockholders—to report to them information they're entitled to.

But just how much information do the debtholders and stockholders really need? How much are they legally entitled to?

These are very difficult questions to answer in straightforward and clear-cut terms. Beyond certain basic facts, exactly what should be put in a footnote to comply with the standard of adequate disclosure is not always clear and definite.

Too little disclosure, such as withholding information about a major lawsuit against the business, would be misleading, and the top executives of the business would be liable for such lack of disclosure. Beyond the legal minimum, which should be insisted on by the company's CPA auditors, footnote disclosure rules and guidelines are somewhat vague and murky.

Managers have rather broad freedom of choice regarding how frank to be and how to express what they put in footnotes. Quite clearly, footnotes are not written like newspaper articles. If the company's advertising copy were written like its footnotes, the business wouldn't make many sales.

Accounting Issues

There is a very serious financial reporting problem regarding the readability of footnotes. As an author I may be overly sensitive to this, but I think not. Investors and securities analysts complain about the dense fog in footnotes. Footnote writing can be so obtuse that you have to suspect that the writing is deliberately obscure. The rules require footnotes, but the rules fail to demand that the footnotes be clear and concise so that an average financial report reader can understand them.

Frequently, the sentence structure of footnotes seems intentionally legalistic and awkward. Technical terminology abounds in footnotes. Poor writing seems more prevalent in footnotes on sensitive matters, such as lawsuits or ventures that the business abandoned with heavy losses. A lack of candor is obvious in many footnotes.

Creditors and stockholders cannot expect managers to expose all the dirty linen of the business in footnotes, or to confess all their bad decisions. But, better clarity and more frankness certainly would help and should not damage the business.

In short, creditors and investors often are stymied by poorly written footnotes. You have only one option, and that is to plow through the underbrush of troublesome footnotes, more than once if necessary. Usually you can tell if particular footnotes are important enough to deserve this extra effort. Beyond this advice, all I can say to you regarding reading footnotes is: "Good luck."

Part Two

FINANCIAL STATEMENT ANALYSIS

16

IMPACT OF GROWTH AND DECLINE ON CASH FLOW

Setting the Stage for Cash Flow Analysis

Chapter 13 explains how to get from net income (the bottom line of the income statement) to the cash flow yield from net income (in the first section of the statement of cash flows). Cash flow can be higher or lower than net income for the period. Why? There are three main reasons: (1) depreciation (and any other noncash expenses and losses recorded in the year), (2) changes in operating assets, and (3) changes in operating liabilities.

1. ***Depreciation (and Other Noncash Expenses and Losses):*** Sales revenue reimburses a business for the expenses it incurs in making sales. Profit is the margin of sales revenue in excess of expenses. One expense is *depreciation*. A business records depreciation expense each period by writing down the cost balance of its property, plant, and equipment (except land). There is no cash outlay in recording this expense. Therefore, depreciation is an "add back" to net income for determining cash flow.

   In addition to depreciation, a business may record other *noncash* expenses and losses. For example, a company may record *amortization* expense to recognize the loss of value of its intangible assets. Or, a business may record an uninsured loss that occurred during the year. Neither asset write down involves a decrease in cash. Therefore, amortization expense and asset write-down losses are added back to net income (just like depreciation).

2. ***Operating Assets:*** Changes in a company's operating assets (accounts receivable, inventory, and prepaid expenses) affect cash flow from profit. An accounts receivable increase delays cash inflow, and increases in other operating assets require cash outflow. In contrast, an accounts receivable decrease accelerates cash inflow, and decreases in other operating assets generate cash. The business, in effect, liquidates part of its investments in these operating assets.

3. ***Operating Liabilities:*** Increases in operating liabilities (accounts payable, accrued expenses payable, and income tax payable) help cash flow during the year. The business avoids cash outlay to the extent of the increases. In other words, part of total expenses for the year are not paid but instead are recorded by increases in these liabilities. Decreases in operating liabilities have the opposite effect: More cash is paid out than the amount of expenses for the year, because the liabilities were paid down.

Caution: Simply adding back depreciation (plus any other noncash expenses and losses) to net income does not give you a true measure of cash flow from operating activities (profit). Changes in operating assets and liabilities during the year cause impacts on cash flow, which can be very sizable in some cases.

Cash Flows in the Steady-State Case

Let's look ahead to next year for the business example that I've used throughout the book. In broad terms, the company's sales revenue next year will hold steady, grow, or decline. These are three basic scenarios for next year. The scenarios have remarkably different impacts on cash flow from operating activities (cash flow from profit).

We start with the steady-state or no-growth/no-decline scenario for the business example. Exhibit 16.1 on this page presents the first section of the company's cash flows statement for next year for the steady-state situation. Sales revenue and expenses in this scenario duplicate the year just ended. I don't bother to present its income statement for the coming year (it's a carbon copy as the one in Exhibit 12.2, which you can refer to).

Realistically, a company's sales revenue and expenses next year will almost certainly change, at least a little bit. My purpose here, however, is to provide a useful point of departure before moving on to the growth and decline scenarios.

Exhibit 16.1 rests on one key premise—that the company's operating assets and liabilities hold steady next year. For example, the company's sales revenue next year is the same as the previous year, so there is no reason for its accounts receivable to change. Likewise, cost of goods sold expense remains the same next year, so there is no reason for the company's inventory to increase or decrease. And likewise for prepaid expenses, accounts payable, accrued expenses payable, and income tax payable. Therefore, Exhibit 16.1 shows zero changes for its operating

assets and liabilities. The only cash flow adjustment to net income, consequently, is the add back for depreciation expense.

Exhibit 16.1 highlights the unique nature of depreciation. The exhibit makes this particular expense stick out like a sore thumb, doesn't it?

Notice those zeros in Exhibit 16.1, representing no changes in the company's operating assets and liabilities. For instance, in this example the company's accounts receivable equals five weeks of annual sales revenue, its inventory equals 13 weeks of annual

EXHIBIT 16.1—CASH FLOW FROM OPERATING (PROFIT-MAKING) ACTIVITIES IN STEADY-STATE SCENARIO
Dollar Amounts in Thousands

Net Income	$2,642
Accounts Receivable Change	0
Inventory Change	0
Prepaid Expenses Change	0
Depreciation Expense	785
Accounts Payable Change	0
Accrued Expenses Change	0
Income Tax Payable Change	0
Cash Flow from Operating Activities	$3,427

cost of goods sold expense, and so on. These ratios can change over time, of course. But in this scenario all the operating ratios of sales revenue and expenses with their corresponding assets and liabilities are held constant for the coming year.

I must admit that even in a steady-state situation the business may allow its average accounts receivable collection period to drift up to six weeks of annual sales, in which case its accounts receivable would increase. This increase would cause a negative cash flow adjustment to net income. In short, even when sales revenue and expenses remain constant next year, a company's operating assets and liabilities may change because the average credit period extended to its customers may change, or its average inventory holding period may change, or its average credit period of accounts payable may change, and so on.

In summary, cash flow from profit in a steady-state scenario is like milking a cow that gives a dependable, steady supply of cash flow every period, equal to depreciation (and other noncash expenses) plus net income. Indeed, the term "cash cow" is used to describe a business in a steady-state situation.

Now, keep in mind that the cash flow from recapturing the capital invested in a company's fixed assets (i.e., the depreciation add back year by year) provides a source of money for replacing fixed assets. Due to inflation over the years, the new fixed assets will cost more than the historical cost of the fixed assets.

Cash Flow Growth Penalty

Growth is the central strategy of most businesses. The purpose of growth, of course, is to increase profit and shareholders' wealth. Without good management, however, expenses can grow faster than sales revenue, and profit may actually decrease. In tough times, just holding its own may be the best a business can do.

Exhibit 16.2 on the next page presents a growth scenario for our business example for the coming year. The exhibit begins on the left with the income statement for the year just ended and shows the budgeted changes in sales revenue and expenses for the coming year. The company is planning for significant growth in sales revenue and profit next year. The CEO wants to know how this growth will impact the company's cash flow from profit next year. (We do not go into how the company arrived at these budgeted changes; we trust that the company's managers have done realistic forecasting and have set achievable goals for next year, which might or might not be entirely true.)

In Exhibit 16.2 the budgeted changes in sales revenue and expenses for the coming year are connected with their cash flow adjustments to net income for next year. See the several lines of connection leading from the changes in the income statement into the cash flow from operating activities section of the cash flows statement.

Note: The amounts of the changes in operating assets and liabilities assume that the company's operating ratios remain the same in the coming year. For instance, notice that cost of goods sold expense is budgeted to increase $4,225,000 next year. In our business example, inventory equals 13 weeks of annual cost of goods sold. So, the increase in cost of goods sold expense causes the amount invested in inventory to increase accordingly:

$$\begin{array}{c}\$4,225,000 \text{ Cost} \\ \text{of Goods Sold} \\ \text{Expense Increase}\end{array} \times \frac{13}{52} = \begin{array}{c}\$1,056,000 \\ \text{Inventory Increase} \\ \text{(Rounded)}\end{array}$$

In like manner, all other operating ratios in the business example are held constant in the growth scenario shown in Exhibit 16.2. Depreciation expense is not based on an operating ratio; rather, depreciation for the coming year is calculated from detailed schedules of the company's fixed assets. This expense is budgeted to increase $95,000 next year because the company is planning to buy new fixed assets. Therefore, the depreciation add back to net income is $880,000 next year ($785,000 + $95,000 = $880,00).

Profit is budgeted to increase $395,000 next year (see Exhibit 16.2), which is a 15% increase over last year. The shareowners should be pleased, of course. But if they anticipate that the business will also increase cash dividends 15%, they may be disappointed. Last year the business generated $3,105,000 cash flow from profit (from Exhibit 13.1). In the growth scenario, however, notice that cash flow does *not* increase with the budgeted profit increase. Cash flow from profit is only $2,731,000 (see Exhibit 16.2). How do you like that?

EXHIBIT 16.2—CASH FLOW FROM OPERATING (PROFIT-MAKING) ACTIVITIES IN GROWTH SCENARIO
Dollar Amounts in Thousands

INCOME STATEMENT

	Actual for Year Just Ended	Budgeted Changes for Next Year		Budgeted Cash Flow from Operating Activities for Next Year	
Sales Revenue	$52,000	$6,500		Budgeted Net Income	$ 3,037
Cost of Goods Sold Expense	33,800	4,225		Accounts Receivable Increase	(625)
Gross Margin	$18,200			Inventory Increase	(1,056)
Selling, General, and Administrative Expenses	12,480	1,560		Prepaid Expenses Increase	(120)
Depreciation Expense	785	95		Depreciation Expense	880
Earnings before Interest and Income Tax	$ 4,935			Accounts Payable Increase	415
Interest Expense	545	35		Accrued Expenses Payable Increase	185
Earnings before Income Tax	$ 4,390			Income Tax Payable Increase	15
Income Tax Expense	1,748	190		Cash Flow from Operating Activities	$ 2,731
Net Income	$ 2,642	$ 395			
Budgeted Increase Next Year	$ 395				
Budgeted Net Income for Next Year	$ 3,037				

The lower amount of cash flow from profit (compared with the year just ended) is caused by the rather large hits on cash flow resulting from the increases in accounts receivable and inventory next year that are needed to support the higher level of sales and expenses. These sizable negative cash flow adjustments to net income are offset to some extent by increases in operating liabilities. In short, profit goes up but cash flow from profit goes down!

There's no such thing as a free lunch for growth when it comes to cash flow. Growth should be good for profit next year, but growth almost always puts a dent in cash flow for the year. In other words, growth does not produce an instant cash flow increase equal to the increase in profit. Cash flow in all likelihood will decrease compared with the previous year—as it does in our business example. And, almost certainly, cash flow would be lower than in the no-growth/steady-state case.

Compare Exhibit 16.2, which shows $2,731,000 cash flow from profit for the growth scenario, with Exhibit 16.1, which shows cash flow from profit in the steady-state scenario. Cash flow is $3,427,000 in the steady-state case, which is $696,000 higher. Of course profit is lower in the steady-state case, but cash flow is higher.

I don't mean to suggest that a business should sacrifice growth to keep its cash flow higher. I do want to make clear, however, that a business pays a cash flow penalty in the short run for growth. During a rapid growth phase, most companies suspend cash dividends to shareowners. All profit is plowed back or reinvested in the business.

A business could speed up cash flow from profit if it were able to improve its operating ratios, such as holding a smaller stock of products in inventory. However, improving operating ratios is generally very difficult in a period of growth. If anything, a business may be under pressure and allow its operating ratios to slip a little. For example, the company may offer customers more liberal credit terms to stimulate sales, which would extend the average accounts receivable credit period. Or the business may increase the size and mix of its inventory to improve delivery times to customers and to provide better selection.

Note: Exhibit 16.2 does not report the company's other sources of cash flow or how it plans to use its cash flow during the coming year. In other words, the *investing* and *financing* sections of the cash flow statement are not presented. (Review Chapter 14 for an explanation of these cash flow sources and uses.) We don't see, for instance, how much the business is planning to spend on capital expenditures next year, or how much the company plans to distribute in cash dividends to its stockholders next year.

Cash Flow Reward from Decline

The old saying "what goes up must come down" certainly applies to most businesses. Few can keep growing forever; the majority eventually slow down or reverse direction. Of course there are cases of remarkable long-run sustained growth; Wal-Mart comes to mind, for instance. But even stalwarts such as McDonald's have slowed down, leveled off, or declined. Some industries are cyclical by nature; their sales revenue goes up and down like a roller coaster over the business cycle.

Profit performance almost always suffers in a decline. It's very difficult for a business to respond to a falloff in sales by cutting its expenses immediately. For one thing, businesses are saddled with *fixed costs* that cannot be reduced in the short run when sales volume declines. A business has to carry out major surgery to reduce these fixed costs. What happens to cash flow from profit (operating activities) when a business suffers a decline in sales?

Note: In Exhibit 16.3 selling, general, and administrative expenses decrease proportionally with sales revenue. Most businesses are saddled with fixed operating costs. A business may not be able to reduce its fixed costs right away when sales start to drop. The company needs more time to ratchet down its fixed costs.

However, the company's selling, general, and administrative expenses do not decrease proportionally with the decrease in sales revenue, mainly because of the fixed-cost nature of many components in this category. Even though its sales drop by a significant percentage, the business cannot immediately reduce many of its fixed costs.

The company's net income is budgeted to drop $450,000 in the decline scenario (see Exhibit 16.3 again). This is bad news, of course. Net income would drop to $2,192,000. But cash flow from profit would be more than $4 million! You may find this rather surprising. In fact, you may even find this hard to believe. So, let me explain why.

The scenario presented in Exhibit 16.3 assumes that the company does not change any of its operating ratios. For example, the ratio of accounts receivable to annual sales revenue remains at five weeks. Since sales revenue drops $6,500,000, accounts receivable drops $625,000:

$$\underset{\substack{\text{Sales Revenue} \\ \text{Decrease}}}{\$6,500,000} \times \frac{5}{52} = \underset{\substack{\text{Accounts Receivable} \\ \text{Decrease}}}{\$625,000}$$

In Exhibit 16.3 every operating asset and liability falls—including income tax payable because the business is budgeting a taxable income decrease next year.

In most respects, the decline scenario (Exhibit 16.3) is the reverse (i.e., mirror image) of the growth scenario (Exhibit 16.2). For example, in the growth scenario the $1,056,000 inventory increase is a negative adjustment to net income, but in the decline scenario the $1,056,000 inventory decrease is a positive adjustment to net income.

In the decline scenario, the business would realize a substantial cash flow from profit and would have to decide what to do

EXHIBIT 16.3—CASH FLOW FROM OPERATING (PROFIT-MAKING) ACTIVITIES IN DECLINE SCENARIO

Dollar Amounts in Thousands

INCOME STATEMENT

	Actual for Year Just Ended	Budgeted Changes for Next Year		Budgeted Cash Flow from Operating Activities for Next Year	
Sales Revenue	$52,000	$(6,500)		Budgeted Net Income	$2,192
Cost of Goods Sold Expense	33,800	(4,225)		Accounts Receivable Decrease	625
Gross Margin	$18,200			Inventory Decrease	1,056
Selling, General, and Administrative Expenses	12,480	(1,560)		Prepaid Expenses Decrease	120
Depreciation Expense	785	0		Depreciation Expense	785
Earnings before Interest and Income Tax	$ 4,935			Accounts Payable Decrease	(415)
Interest Expense	545	(25)		Accrued Expenses Payable Decrease	(175)
Earnings before Income Tax	$ 4,390			Income Tax Payable Decrease	(45)
Income Tax Expense	1,748	(240)		Cash Flow from Operating Activities	$4,143
Net Income	$ 2,642	$ (450)			
Budgeted Decrease Next Year	$ (450)				
Budgeted Net Income for Next Year	$ 2,192				

with the cash. The company could pay down its debt (interest-bearing liabilities), or possibly retire some of its capital stock shares. If the business predicts that the decline will be permanent, it should not need as much capital from debt and equity sources. At the lower level of sales, the company can get by on a lower level of assets, which means it needs less capital.

The broader challenge facing a business that suffers a serious downturn is developing a rebound strategy. Downsizing a business, particularly laying off employees who have been with the company many years, is painful for everyone. Downsizing means management has thrown in the towel and has given up on finding alternatives for maintaining the size of the business.

Red Ink and Cash Flow

Following our discussion of business decline in the preceding section, this is a good place to bring up an unpleasant subject. What happens to cash flow when the bottom line of the income statement is in red ink? In other words, what happens to cash flow when a business records a *net loss* for the year?

A net loss means that the total of expenses and losses is more than sales revenue (and income if any) for the year. Suppose a business records $10 million net loss for the year; did its cash decrease $10 million during the year? No, the cash impact from the net loss is bound to be different. To determine cash flow, you apply the same cash flow adjustments that are explained in Chapter 13. And there is another factor to consider in many red ink cases.

A large net loss for the year may be due to huge write-downs of assets (or by recording a large liability). For example, the balance in a company's goodwill asset account may be written down because the asset suffered what is called *impairment*. This means that management has come to the conclusion that the asset has a lower future value to the business, or perhaps no

value at all. The asset write-down does not involve a cash outlay. So, cash flow from operating activities is not hurt by such an asset write-down. Many financial institutions were recording huge write-downs of their subprime mortgage loan receivables as I was revising this book.

Suppose that a business records no asset write-downs (or liability write-ups) during the year, but reports a sizable net loss for the year. Its cash flow from operating activities could very well be negative. In other words, the total cash outlays for expenses could be more than total cash inflow from sales revenue, even after the depreciation add back is considered. This condition is called *negative cash flow*.

In a negative cash flow situation, a business is using up its available cash. The rate at which the business is using up its cash is called the *burn rate*. The burn rate can be used to estimate how long the business can live without a major cash infusion. Start-up business ventures typically experience negative operating cash flow during their first few years. Often their burn rate is too high and they don't make it.

Final Comment

Financial reporting standards do not require a business to explain or comment on its cash flow strategies and problems. The life or death of the business is at stake, but top management may not say anything about how they expect to deal with their serious cash flow problems. Chapter 17 explains financial statement ratios that help lenders and investors identify liquidity and solvency problems of a business.

17

FINANCIAL STATEMENT RATIOS

Purpose of Financial Statements

The main purpose of financial reporting is to provide up-to-date financial information about a business to its investors and lenders, who are its sources of capital and have a right to and need for the information. Others also may be interested in the financial affairs of a business—for example, its employees and its other creditors. When they read the financial report, they should keep in mind that financial reports are directed to the owner-investors of the business and its lenders. Financial reporting standards have been developed with this primary audience in mind.

According to estimates, there are about 10,000 publicly owned businesses in the United States. Their capital stock shares and other securities are traded in public markets. The dissemination of financial information by these companies is governed by federal law, which is enforced mainly by the Securities and Exchange Commission (SEC). The New York Stock Exchange, Nasdaq, and other securities markets also enforce many rules and regulations regarding the release and communication of financial information by companies whose securities are traded on their markets.

Securities of some 12,000 foreign businesses are traded in stock markets around the world. Each country has its own government enforcement agencies. The European Union (EU) regulates financial reporting by its member states. Almost all countries, including the United States, are moving rapidly toward adopting a set of *international financial reporting and accounting standards*, which I discuss in Chapter 19.

In the United States and other countries, a business cannot legally release information to some stockholders or lenders but not to others, nor can a business tip off some of them before informing the others. The laws and accepted standards of financial reporting are designed to ensure that all stockholders and lenders have equal access to a company's financial information and financial reports.

A company's financial report may not be the first source of information about its profit performance. In the United States, most public corporations issue press releases of their most recent earnings results. These press releases precede mailing the hard copy of the company's financial report to its stockholders and lenders. Most public companies put their financial reports on their web sites at the time of or soon after the press releases. Private businesses do not usually send out letters to their owners and lenders in advance of their financial reports, although they could, of course. Also, private companies generally do not put their financial reports on their publicly accessible web sites.

This chapter examines what stockholders and lenders do with financial statements once they have access to them. The chapter centers on the *annual* financial statements. (Quarterly financial reports are abbreviated versions of the annual reports.) In particular, this chapter focuses on certain *ratios* that are useful to investors and lenders.

Overview of Financial Statements

Exhibit 17.1 presents a company's annual financial statements. This is the same company example used throughout earlier chapters. The footnotes for these statements are not included. (Chapter 15 discusses footnotes to financial statements.)

The company in this example is privately owned, which means its capital stock shares are not traded in a public market. The business has about 50 shareholders; some are managers of the business, including the CEO, the president, and several vice presidents. A business this size could go into the public marketplace for equity capital through an initial public offering (IPO) of capital stock shares and become publicly owned. However, the company has decided to remain private.

This chapter does not pretend to cover the broad field of *securities analysis* (i.e., the analysis of stocks and debt instruments issued by corporations). This broad field includes the analysis of competitive advantages and disadvantages of a business, domestic and international economic developments, business combination possibilities, and much more. The key ratios explained in this chapter are basic building blocks in securities analysis.

Also, this chapter does not discuss the important topic of *trend analysis*, which involves comparing a company's latest financial statements with its previous years' statements to identify important year-to-year changes. For example, investors and lenders are very interested in the sales growth or decline of a business, and the resulting impact on profit performance, cash flow, and financial condition. (Chapter 16 examines the impact of growth and decline on cash flow.)

This chapter has a more modest objective—to explain basic ratios used in financial statement analysis. Only a handful of ratios are discussed in the chapter, but they are widely used. So far only two financial statement ratios have been mentioned: the *accounts receivable turnover ratio* in Chapter 4 and the *inventory turnover ratio* in Chapter 5. This chapter explains a few more ratios that are very useful to lenders and investors.

Upon opening a company's financial report, probably one of the first things most investors do is to give the financial statements a once-over; they do a fairly quick scan of the financial statements. What do they look for? In my experience, they look first at the bottom line of the income statement, to see if the business made a profit or suffered a loss for the year.

As one sports celebrity put it when explaining how he keeps tabs on his various business investments, he looks first to see if the bottom line has "parentheses around it." The business in our example does not; it avoided a loss. Its income statement reports that the business earned $2,642,000 net income for the year. Is this profit performance good, mediocre, or poor? Ratios help answer this question.

EXHIBIT 17.1—EXTERNAL FINANCIAL STATEMENTS OF BUSINESS (WITHOUT FOOTNOTES)

Dollar Amounts in Thousands, Except Earnings per Share

INCOME STATEMENT FOR YEAR

Sales Revenue	$52,000
Cost of Goods Sold Expense	33,800
Gross Margin	$18,200
Selling, General, and	
Administrative Expenses	12,480
Depreciation Expense	785
Earnings before Interest and Tax	$ 4,935
Interest Expense	545
Earnings before Income Tax	$ 4,390
Income Tax Expense	1,748
Net Income	$ 2,642
Basic Earnings per Share	$ 3.30

STATEMENT OF CHANGES IN STOCKHOLDERS' EQUITY FOR YEAR

	Capital Stock	Retained Earnings
Beginning Balances	$7,950	$13,108
Net Income for Year		2,642
Shares Issued during Year	$ 175	
Dividends Paid during Year		(750)
Ending Balances	$8,125	$15,000

BALANCE SHEET AT END OF YEAR

Assets

Cash		$ 3,265
Accounts Receivable		5,000
Inventory		8,450
Prepaid Expenses		960
Current Assets		$17,675
Property, Plant, and Equipment	$16,500	
Accumulated Depreciation	(4,250)	12,250
Intangible Assets		5,575
Total Assets		$35,500

Liabilities and Stockholders' Equity

Accounts Payable		$ 3,320
Accrued Expenses Payable		1,515
Income Tax Payable		165
Short-Term Notes Payable		3,125
Current Liabilities		$ 8,125
Long-Term Notes Payable		4,250
Total Liabilities		$12,375
Capital Stock (800,000 shares)	$ 8,125	
Retained Earnings	15,000	
Stockholders' Equity		$23,125
Total Liabilities and Stockholders' Equity		$35,500

STATEMENT OF CASH FLOWS FOR YEAR

Net Income	$ 2,642
Accounts Receivable Increase	(320)
Inventory Increase	(935)
Prepaid Expenses Increase	(275)
Depreciation Expense	785
Accounts Payable Increase	645
Accrued Expenses Payable Increase	480
Income Tax Payable Increase	83
Cash Flow from Operating Activities	$ 3,105
Expenditures for Property, Plant, and Equipment	$(3,050)
Expenditures for Intangible Assets	(575)
Cash Flow from Investing Activities	(3,625)
Increase in Short-Term Notes Payable	$ 125
Increase in Long-Term Notes Payable	500
Issue of Additional Capital Stock Shares	175
Cash Dividends Paid Shareholders	(750)
Cash Flow from Financing Activities	50
Decrease in Cash during Year	$ (470)
Cash Balance at Start of Year	3,735
Cash Balance at End of Year	3,265

This company does not report any *extraordinary gains or losses* for the year, which are one-time, nonrecurring events. For example, a business may sell a major fixed asset and record a gain. Or a business may record a restructuring charge for the cost of laying off employees who will receive severance packages. These out-of-the-ordinary, unusual gains and losses are reported separately from the ongoing, continuing operations of a company. This topic would lead into a labyrinth of technical details.

But Be Warned: These irregular gains and losses complicate the evaluation and forecasting of profit performance! Extraordinary gains and losses, especially losses, raise very troublesome questions, such as:

- Is an extraordinary loss really a correction of past years' accounting mistakes?

- What if a company reports such irregular gains and losses, in fact, on a recurring basis?

- Will such extraordinary gains and losses happen again in the future, and if so when and how much?

Deciding how to deal with such gains and losses is a vexing challenge, to say the least.

After reading the income statement, most financial statement readers probably take a quick look at the company's assets and compare them with the liabilities of the business. Are the assets adequate to the demands of the company's liabilities? Ratios help answer this question.

Next, the readers take a look at the company's cash flows. As you see, the company's statement of cash flows is included in Exhibit 17.1. This is one of the primary financial statements of a business entity that must be included in its external financial reports. Nevertheless, I almost did not include it in the exhibit, which might surprise you.

None of the ratios discussed in this chapter involve the cash flows statement. There are no benchmark ratios for cash flows. Still, cash flow gets a lot of ink in the financial press and in reports on corporations published by stockbrokers and investment advisors. Cash flow from profit (operating activities) is considered a key variable for a business. The business in our example realized $3,105,000 cash flow from profit (operating activities) for the year just ended, which is less than its $3,625,000 capital expenditures for the year. Its other sources and uses of cash provided only $50,000 cash for the year. Thus, the company's cash balance dropped $470,000 during the year.

Reading the cash flow statement in this manner provides a useful synopsis of where the business got its money during the year and what it did with the money. We could divide cash flow from profit by net income to determine cash flow as a percentage of net income. I think this is an interesting ratio. But it is not one of the benchmark ratios used in financial statement analysis.

We could divide cash flow from profit (operating activities) by the number of capital stock shares to get cash flow per share. But, as I mention in Chapter 14, the Financial Accounting Standards Board (FASB) has specifically discouraged this ratio, which is most unusual. It is quite rare for the FASB to go out of its way to put the kibosh on a particular ratio.

Exhibit 17.1 introduces a new financial statement—the *statement of changes in stockholders' equity*. In some respects this is not really a financial statement; it's more of a supporting schedule that summarizes changes in the capital stock and retained earnings accounts. The business in our example probably would include this statement. However, it is not all that necessary, because the changes in its two stockholders' equity accounts are easy to follow.

The business issued 7,000 additional shares of capital stock during the year; the $175,000 proceeds from issuing the shares are reported in the statement of cash flows (see Exhibit 17.1). So, the balance in its capital stock account increased. Net income for the year increased retained earnings, and the cash dividends paid to stockholders decreased the account.

The statement of changes in stockholders' equity is definitely needed when a business has a complex capitalization (ownership) structure that includes different classes of stock, and when a business repurchases some of its own capital stock shares during the year. This financial statement (schedule) is also needed when a business has certain types of losses and gains that are recorded directly to retained earnings and bypass the income statement.

Exploring these special gains and losses that do not go through the income statement would take us into the technical territory of "comprehensive income," which is beyond the scope of this book. The statement of changes in stockholders' equity is often a very complex and highly technical financial statement to read. Frankly, I usually just skim the statement of changes in stockholders' equity and focus mainly on the big three financial statements (balance sheet, income statement, and cash flows statement).

Debt-Paying Ability, Liquidity, and Solvency Ratios

Stock analysts, investment managers, individual investors, investment bankers, economists, and others are interested in three key financial aspects of a business—cash flows, solvency, and profit performance. Cash flow analysis does not use ratios (at least not yet). In contrast, the analysis of solvency and profit performance makes use of several benchmark ratios.

Bankers and other lenders when deciding whether to make and renew loans to a business direct their attention to certain financial statement ratios. These ratios provide a useful financial profile of the business in assessing its creditworthiness and in judging the ability of the business to repay its loans and pay interest on time.

Solvency refers to the ability of a business to pay its liabilities when they come due. Maintaining solvency (debt-paying ability) is essential for every business. If a business defaults on its debt obligations, it becomes vulnerable to legal proceedings that could stop the company in its tracks, or at least could interfere with its normal operations.

Note: From here forward in the chapter all dollar amounts from the financial statements are in thousands (as they are in Exhibit 17.1). Instead of reminding you every time where I show the calculation of a ratio, I assume that you understand that the relevant data is taken from Exhibit 17.1.

The Current Ratio: Test of Short-Term Solvency

The *current ratio* tests the short-term liability-paying ability of a business. It is calculated by dividing total current assets by total current liabilities in a company's most recent balance sheet. The current ratio for the company is computed as follows:

$$\frac{\$17,675 \text{ Current Assets}}{\$8,125 \text{ Current Liabilities}} = 2.18 \text{ Current Ratio}$$

The current ratio is hardly ever expressed as a percent (which would be 218% in this company example). The current ratio for the business is stated as 2.18 to 1.00, or more simply just as 2.18.

The general rule, or standard, is that the current ratio for a business should be 2 to 1 or higher. Most businesses find that this minimum current ratio is expected by their creditors. In other words, short-term creditors generally like to see a business limit its current liabilities to one-half or less of its current assets.

Why do short-term creditors put this limit on a business? The main reason is to provide a safety cushion of protection for the payment of its short-term liabilities. A current ratio of 2 to 1 means there is $2 of cash and assets that should be converted into cash during the near future that will be available to pay each

$1 of current liabilities that come due in roughly the same time period. Each dollar of short-term liabilities is backed up with two dollars of cash on hand or near-term cash inflows. The extra dollar of current assets provides a margin of safety for the creditors.

A company could possibly pay its liabilities on time with a current ratio less than 2 to 1, or perhaps even if its current ratio were as low as 1 to 1. In this example, the company's three non-interest-bearing liabilities—accounts payable, accrued expenses payable, and income tax payable—equal 28% of its total current assets. In addition, its banker has lent the business $3,125,000 on the basis of short-term loans, which is 18% of its total current assets. Its short-term lenders may not be willing to lend the business very much more—although perhaps the business could persuade its banker to go up to, say, $4 million or $5 million on short-term notes payable.

In summary, short-term sources of credit generally demand that a company's current assets be double its current liabilities. After all, creditors are not owners—they don't share in the profit earned by the business. The income on their loans is limited to the interest they charge (and collect). As creditors, they quite properly minimize their loan risks; as limited-income (fixed-income) investors, they are not compensated to take on much risk.

The Acid Test Ratio (Quick Ratio)

Inventory is many weeks away from conversion into cash. Products are usually held two, three, or four months before being sold. If sales are made on credit, which is normal when one business sells to another business, there is a second waiting period before the receivables are collected. In short, inventory is not nearly as liquid as accounts receivable; it takes a lot longer to convert inventory into cash. Furthermore, there's no guarantee that all the products in inventory will be sold.

A more severe measure of the short-term liability-paying ability of a business is the *acid test ratio*, which excludes inventory (and prepaid expenses also). Only cash, short-term marketable securities investments (if any), and accounts receivable are counted as sources to pay the current liabilities of the business.

This ratio is also called the *quick ratio* because only cash and assets quickly convertible into cash are included in the amount available for paying current liabilities. It's more in the nature of a liquidity ratio that focuses on how much cash and near-cash assets a business possesses to pay all of its short-term liabilities.

In this example, the company's acid test ratio is calculated as follows (the business has no investments in marketable securities):

$$\frac{\$3,265 \text{ Cash} + \$5,000 \text{ Accounts Receivable}}{\$8,125 \text{ Current Liabilities}} = 1.02 \text{ Acid Test Ratio}$$

The general rule is that a company's acid test ratio should be 1 to 1 or better, although you find many exceptions.

Debt to Equity Ratio

Some debt is generally good, but too much debt is dangerous. The *debt to equity ratio* is an indicator of whether a company is using debt prudently, or perhaps has gone too far and is overburdened with debt that may likely cause problems. For this example, the company's debt to equity ratio calculation is:

$$\frac{\$12,375 \text{ Total Liabilities}}{\$23,125 \text{ Total Stockholders Equity}} = .54 \text{ Debt to Equity Ratio}$$

This ratio tells us that the company is using $.54 of liabilities in addition to each $1.00 of stockholders' equity in the business. Notice that all liabilities (non-interest-bearing as well as interest-bearing, and both short-term and long-term) are included in this ratio, and that all owners' equity (invested capital stock and retained earnings) is included.

This business—with its .54 debt ratio—would be viewed as moderately leveraged. *Leverage* refers to using the equity capital base to raise additional capital from nonowner sources. In other words, the business is using $1.54 of total capital for every $1.00 of equity capital. The business has $1.54 of assets working for it for every dollar of equity capital in the business.

Most businesses stay below a 1 to 1 debt to equity ratio. They don't want to take on too much debt, or they cannot convince lenders to put up more than one-half of their assets. However, some capital-intensive (asset-heavy) businesses such as public utilities and financial institutions operate with debt to equity ratios much higher than 1 to 1. In other words, they are highly leveraged.

Times Interest Earned Ratio

To pay interest on its debt, a business needs to have sufficient earnings before interest and (income) tax (EBIT). To test the ability to pay interest from earnings, the *times interest earned ratio* is calculated. Annual earnings before interest and income tax is divided by interest expense:

$$\frac{\$4{,}935 \text{ EBIT}}{\$545 \text{ Interest Expense}} = \begin{array}{l} 9.1 \text{ Times Interest} \\ \text{Earned Ratio} \end{array}$$

There is no standard or general rule for this particular ratio—although obviously the ratio should be higher than 1 to 1. In this example, the company's EBIT is more than 9 times its annual interest expense, which is comforting from the lender's point of view. Lenders would be very alarmed if a business barely covers its annual interest expense. (The company's management should be equally alarmed, of course.)

Return on Sales and Return on Equity Ratios

Making sales while controlling expenses is how a business makes profit. The profit residual slice from a company's total sales revenue pie is expressed by the *return on sales ratio*, which is profit divided by sales revenue for the period. The company's return on sales ratio for its latest year is:

$$\frac{\$2,642 \text{ Net Income}}{\$52,000 \text{ Sales Revenue}} = 5.1\% \text{ Return on Sales Ratio}$$

There is another way of explaining the return on sales ratio. For each $100 of sales revenue, the business earned $5.10 net income—and had expenses of $94.90. Return on sales varies quite markedly from one industry to another. Some businesses do well with only a 1% or 2% return on sales; others need more than 10% to justify the large amount of capital invested in their assets.

Owners take the risk of whether their business can earn a profit and sustain its profit performance over the years. How much would you pay for a business that consistently suffers a loss? The value of the owners' investment depends first and foremost on the past and potential future profit performance of the business—or not just profit, I should say, but profit relative to the capital invested to earn that profit.

For instance, suppose a business earns $100,000 annual net income for its stockholders. If its stockholders' equity is only $250,000, then its profit performance relative to the stockholders' capital used to make that profit is 40%, which is very good

indeed. If, however, stockholders' equity is $2,500,000, then the company's profit performance is 4%, which is terrible relative to the owners' capital tied up in the business to earn that profit.

The point is that profit should be compared with the amount of capital invested to earn the profit. Profit for a period divided by the amount of capital invested to earn that profit is called *return on investment* (ROI). ROI is a broad concept that applies to almost any sort of investment of capital.

The owners' investment in a business is the total of the owners' equity accounts in the company's balance sheet. Their profit is bottom-line net income for the period, less dividends that have to be paid on any preferred capital stock shares issued by the business. Preferred stock shares have a first claim on net income. In this example, the business has issued only one class of stock shares; the company has no preferred stock, so all of net income belongs to its common stockholders.

Dividing annual net income by stockholders' equity gives the *return on equity* (ROE) ratio. The calculation for the company's ROE in this example is:

$$\frac{\$2,642 \text{ Net Income}}{\$23,125 \text{ Stockholders' Equity}} = \frac{11.4\% \text{ Return}}{\text{on Equity Ratio}}$$

Note: The ending balance of stockholders' equity is used to simplify the analysis. Alternatively, the weighted average during the year could be used, especially if there are significant changes during the year.

By most standards, the company's 11.4% annual ROE would be acceptable but not impressive. However, everything is relative. ROE should be compared with industrywide averages and with investment alternatives. Also, the risk factor is important; just how risky is the stockholders' capital investment in the business?

We need to know much more about the history and prospects of the business to reach a conclusion regarding whether its 11.4% ROE is good, mediocre, or poor. Also, we would have to consider the opportunity cost of capital—that is, what ROI could be earned by the stockholders on alternative uses for their capital. And we have not considered the income tax factor. Judging ROE is not a simple matter!

Another useful ratio to calculate is the following:

$$\frac{\$4,935 \text{ EBIT}}{\$35,500 \text{ Total Assets}} = \frac{13.9\% \text{ Return on}}{\text{Assets Ratio}}$$

This *return on assets* (ROA) ratio reveals that the business earned $13.90 before interest and income tax expenses on each $100 of assets. The ROA is compared with the annual interest rate on the company's borrowed money. In this example, the company's annual interest rate on its short-term and long-term debt is 7.5%. The business earned 13.9% on the money borrowed, as measured by the ROA. The difference or spread between the two rates is a favorable 6.4%. This source of profit enhancement is called *financial leverage gain*. In contrast, if a company's ROA is less than its interest rate, it suffers a financial leverage loss.

Earnings per Share (EPS) and Price/Earnings (P/E) Ratios

The capital stock shares of 10,000 domestic business corporations are traded in public markets—the New York Stock Exchange, Nasdaq, and other stock exchanges in the United States. The day-to-day market price changes of these shares receive a great deal of attention, to say the least! More than any other single factor, the market value of capital stock shares depends on the net income (earnings) performance of a business—its past profit performance and its future profit potential.

Suppose I tell you that the market price of a stock is $60, and ask you whether this value is too high or too low, or just about right. You could compare the market price with the stockholders' equity per share reported in the balance sheet—called the *book value per share*. This is an asset-based valuation approach. The company's total assets minus its total liabilities equal its stockholders' equity. The asset-based or book value method has a respectable history in securities analysis. Today, however, the asset-based approach plays second fiddle to the earnings-based approach. The starting point is to calculate earnings (net income) per share.

Earnings per Share (EPS)

One of the most widely used ratios in stock value and securities analysis is *earnings per share* (EPS). The essential calculation of earnings per share is as follows:

$$\frac{\$2{,}642 \text{ Net Income Available for Common Stockholders}}{800{,}000 \text{ Shares of Common Stock Outstanding}} = \$3.30 \text{ Basic Earnings per Share}$$

Note: To be technical, the weighted average number of shares outstanding during the year should be used—which takes into account that some shares may have been issued and outstanding only part of the year and that the business may have reduced the number of its outstanding shares during part of the year.

First, notice that the numerator (top number) in the ratio is *net income available for common stockholders*, which equals bottom-line net income less any dividends paid to the preferred stockholders of the business. Many business corporations issue preferred stock that requires a fixed amount of dividends to be paid each year. The mandatory annual dividends to the preferred stockholders are deducted from net income to determine net income available for the common stockholders. (The preferred stock dividends are not reported as an expense; net income is before any dividends to stockholders.)

Second, please notice the word *basic* in front of *earnings per share*, which means that the actual number of common stock shares in the hands of stockholders is the denominator (bottom number) in the EPS calculation. Many business corporations have entered into contracts of one sort or another that require the company at some time in the future to issue additional stock shares at prices below the market value of its stock shares. But none of these shares have been actually issued yet.

For example, business corporations award managers *stock options* to buy common stock shares of the company at fixed prices. If in the future the market value of the shares rises over the fixed option prices, the managers will exercise their rights and buy capital stock shares at a bargain price. With stock options, therefore, the number of stock shares is subject to inflation. When (and if) the additional shares are issued, EPS will suffer because net income will have to be spread over a larger number of stock shares. EPS will be diluted, or thinned down, because of the larger denominator in the EPS ratio.

Basic EPS does not recognize the additional shares that will be issued when stock options are exercised. Also, basic EPS does not take into account potential dilution effects of any convertible bonds and convertible preferred stock that have been issued by a business. These securities can be converted at the option of the security holders into common stock shares at predetermined prices.

To warn investors of the potential effects of stock options and convertible securities, a second EPS is reported by public corporations, which is called *diluted* EPS. This lower EPS takes into account the dilution effects caused by issuing additional common stock shares under stock option plans, convertible securities, and any other commitments a business has entered into that could require it to issue additional stock shares at predetermined prices in the future.

Basic EPS and diluted EPS (if applicable) must be reported in the income statements of publicly owned business corporations. This indicates the importance of EPS. In contrast, none of the other ratios discussed in this chapter have to be reported, although many public companies report selected ratios.

Price/Earnings (P/E) Ratio

The market price of stock shares of a public business corporation is compared with EPS and expressed in the *price/earnings (P/E) ratio* as follows:

$$\frac{\text{Current Market Price of Stock Shares}}{\text{Earnings per Share}} = \frac{\text{Price}}{\text{Earnings Ratio}}$$

Suppose a public company's stock shares are trading at $40 per share and its basic EPS for the most recent year (called the trailing 12 months) is $2. (The company does not report a diluted EPS.) Thus, its P/E ratio is 20. Like other ratios discussed in this chapter, the P/E ratio should be compared with industrywide and marketwide averages to judge whether it is acceptable, too high, or too low. I remember when a P/E ratio of 8 was considered right. As I write this sentence, however, P/E ratios in the range of 15 to 18 are considered acceptable and nothing to be alarmed about.

Now, here's a problem in calculating the P/E ratio for a company: Should you use its *basic* EPS or its *diluted* EPS? If the business reports only basic EPS there is no problem, of course. But when a public company reports both, which EPS should you use? Well, it is done both ways. My best advice is to check the legend in the stock market tables in the *Wall Street Journal* and the *New York Times* to find out which EPS the newspaper uses in reporting the P/E ratios for companies. Using diluted EPS is more conservative; that is, it gives a higher P/E ratio.

The market prices for stock shares of a private business are not available, because the shares are not traded and when they are sold the price is not made public. Nevertheless, stockholders in these businesses are of course interested in what their shares are worth. To estimate the value of stock shares a P/E multiple can be used. In the company example, its EPS is $3.30 for the most recent year (see Exhibit 17.1). Suppose you own some of the capital stock shares, and someone offers to buy your shares. You could establish an offer price at, say, 12 times basic EPS. This would be $39.60 per share. The potential buyer may not be willing to pay this price, or he or she might be willing to pay 15 or 18 times basic EPS.

Market Cap

Suppose the stock shares of a public company are currently trading at $65 per share, and the business has 10 million shares outstanding. The *market cap*, or total market value capitalization of the company, is $650 million ($65 market value per share × 10 million capital stock shares = $650 million). I'd bet you dollars to doughnuts that if you compared the market cap of this business with the shareholders' equity amount reported in its latest balance sheet, the market cap would be much higher. The book value (balance sheet value) of shareholders' equity is the historical record of the amounts invested in the business by the owners in years past plus its retained earnings over the years. Both these numbers may go back many years.

In contrast, if a business is in financial straits, its market cap may be lower than the book value of its owners' equity—at least for the time being.

Final Comments

Many other ratios can be calculated from the data in financial statements. For example, the *asset turnover ratio* (annual sales revenue divided by total assets) and the *dividend yield* (annual cash dividends per share divided by market value per share) are two ratios you often see used in securities analysis. There's no end to the ratios that can be calculated.

The trick is to focus on those ratios that have the most interpretive value. Of course it's not easy to figure out which ratios are the most important. Professional investors tend to use too many ratios rather than too few, in my opinion. But you never know which ratio might provide a valuable clue to the future market value increase or decrease of a stock.

18

PROFIT ANALYSIS FOR BUSINESS MANAGERS

First, a Word about Managerial Accounting

Unless you happened to start reading this book with this chapter, you know that the previous chapters focus on the *external financial statements* reported by businesses. As you probably know, accounting involves more than preparing a company's external financial statements, although this is certainly one of its main functions.

Every business must install an *accounting system*, which includes forms, procedures, records, reports, computer hardware and software, and personnel, to keep the day-to-day operations of a business running smoothly and to prevent delays and stoppages. Every accounting system needs strong *internal controls* to deter and detect errors and potential fraud. Fraud and various other types of dishonesty can plague any business.

Perhaps I needn't remind you, but many different *tax returns* have to be filed on time by every business—for income taxes, property taxes, sales taxes, and payroll taxes. Accountants are in charge of tax compliance in a business. Accountants are the tax experts because tax laws are written in the language of accounting.

Designing accounting systems, complying with tax laws, and preparing external financial reports are three bedrock accounting functions of every business. And the accounting staff in a business has another very important function—providing information to its managers for their decision making, planning, and control. This fourth function of accounting is called *management accounting* or *managerial accounting* (which I prefer).

Managerial accounting is an *internal* function, which is carried out inside a business to help its managers make sound decisions, develop plans and budgets, and exercise control. In short, the purpose of managerial accounting is to help managers be good managers. Managerial accounting, more than anything else, involves providing useful information to managers and helping them use this information in the most effective manner.

The design of internal accounting reports to managers is very dependent on the nature of the business and how the business is organized. Suppose a business is divided into sales territories, for example; accounting reports are needed for each sales territory. Each sales territory may be divided into major product lines; so, the accounting reports separate each product line in each territory. In short, management accounting follows the organizational structure of a business.

External financial statements are designed for the outside, nonmanagement investors and lenders of the business. The external accounting reports of a business do not contain all the financial information its managers need. Managers should understand their company's external financial statements like the backs of their hands. But they need additional accounting reports that provide more information, much of which is confidential and is not released outside the confines of the business.

Accountants present a great deal more information about expenses in internal income statements (profit reports) to managers. Managers need this detailed information for controlling expenses. In addition, managers need to know how expenses behave relative to changes in sales prices and sales volume. All managers having profit responsibility should have a sure-handed analytical grip on how changes in sales volume and sales prices impact their profit performance.

According to this logic, internal profit accounting reports to managers should classify operating expenses according to how they behave relative to changes in sales prices and sales volume. Well, this is good advice, but in actual practice accountants generally do *not* classify expenses this way in internal profit reports to managers. There are many reasons why they don't. For one thing, it would pile more work on top of all the other things accountants do in a business. Also, most managers probably don't ask for expense information classified this way. But I think they're missing the boat on this. After reading this chapter, you'll have to be the judge on this issue.

To illustrate the importance of knowing how expenses behave, let me put a question to you here. Assume that all other factors remain the same next year, except one. Which would be better for profit: a 5% sales price increase across the board, or a 5% sales volume increase on all products and services sold by the business? If you, the business manager, could have one but not the other, which would you choose—the sales price option or the sales volume option? One is clearly better, as I will explain.

A Word of Caution: Before moving on, I should point out that this chapter is not a comprehensive survey of the field of managerial accounting—far from it! I do not discuss budgeting, standard costs, management control reports, cost allocation methods, and several other topics. My more modest goal is to demonstrate how expenses should be classified in internal profit reports to managers, in order to make these accounting reports more useful for their decision-making analysis. I believe business managers will find this chapter very instructive.

Classification of Operating Expenses in Management Profit Reports

To begin, see Exhibit 18.1, which is the exact duplicate of Exhibit 2.2. I repeat it here for ease of reference. This is the *external* income statement of the company example I use throughout earlier chapters.

EXHIBIT 18.1—EXTERNAL INCOME STATEMENT FOR YEAR
Dollar Amounts in Thousands

Sales Revenue	$ 52,000
Cost of Goods Sold Expense	(33,800)
Gross Margin	$ 18,200
Selling, General, and Administrative Expenses	(12,480)
Depreciation Expense	(785)
Earnings before Interest and Income Tax	$ 4,935
Interest Expense	(545)
Earnings before Income Tax	$ 4,390
Income Tax Expense	(1,748)
Net Income	$ 2,642

You see in Exhibit 18.1 the typical format of an external income statement. There's nothing wrong about this income statement format for reporting to the company's outside investors and lenders. As you will notice, the external income statement reports highly condensed, summary-level information.

The first thought that comes to your mind here probably is that managers need a lot of detailed information for controlling the business. Yes, you're quite right. For control purposes, business managers need to keep track of a thousand and one details. Also, managers need to develop relevant benchmarks and focus on "control points." For example, managers should keep a close watch on the total number of employees and sales revenue per employee. Productivity measures are very important for manufacturers. Retailers should measure inventory shrinkage in order to determine the losses from customer shoplifting and employee theft.

I could write an entire book on management control and the detailed information managers need for effective control. I could discuss in some detail the classification of sales revenue and expenses according to the *profit centers* and *cost centers* of a business. A profit center is a separate, identifiable source of sales revenue and matching expenses. For an auto dealer, for instance, one profit center is its new car and truck sales, another is its used car and truck sales, and a third is its service and parts department. A cost center is an organizational unit that does not generate sales revenue, such as the accounting and maintenance departments.

This is not a book on managerial accounting, so I don't delve into the many topics of that branch of accounting. But I do want to make clear that the way operating expenses are reported in external income statements is not satisfactory for internal profit reporting to managers. I don't just mean that managers need more details about operating expenses, although this is true, of course. Rather, the point I want to emphasize here is that operating

EXHIBIT 18.2—MANAGEMENT PROFIT REPORT FOR YEAR

Dollar Amounts in Thousands

Sales Revenue	$ 52,000
Cost of Goods Sold Expense	(33,800)
Gross Margin	$ 18,200
Sales Revenue Sensitive Expenses	(4,420)
Sales Volume Sensitive Expenses	(3,120)
Profit Margin before Fixed Expenses	$ 10,660
Fixed Selling and Operating Expenses	(4,940)
Fixed Depreciation Expense	(785)
Earnings before Interest and Income Tax	$ 4,935
Interest Expense	(545)
Earnings before Income Tax	$ 4,390
Income Tax Expense	(1,748)
Net Income	$ 2,642

expenses should be classified according to how the expenses behave *relative to changes in sales revenue and sales volume*.

Deducting cost of goods sold expense immediately below the sales revenue from the goods sold is very useful in order to determine the *gross margin* from sales (also called *gross profit*). Every business must earn an adequate gross margin to cover its other expenses. Earning a satisfactory bottom-line profit begins with earning an adequate gross margin on sales—there's no doubt about this. Furthermore, reporting interest and income tax as separate expenses in profit reports to managers makes sense. This leaves the question of how operating expenses should be reported in internal profit reports.

Exhibit 18.2, the management profit report for the year, reclassifies the company's operating expenses, which in the external income statement (Exhibit 18.1) are reported as one amount called "selling, general, and administrative expenses." In the management profit report (Exhibit 18.2), these expenses are reclassified into three types:

1. *Sales Revenue Sensitive Expenses*—operating costs that depend on and vary with total sales revenue (the total dollar amount of sales). Sales commissions equal to a certain percent of sales and credit card discounts paid by a retailer to a credit card company are two examples.

2. *Sales Volume Sensitive Expenses*—operating costs that depend on and vary with the total sales volume, or quantities of products and services sold to customers. Packaging and transportation costs are two main examples.

3. *Fixed Selling and Operating Expenses*—costs that are relatively fixed in amount and cannot be changed over the short run. Employees on fixed salaries, building rent, equipment lease payments, and property taxes are examples

of fixed operating costs. These fixed costs can be reduced given enough time, but are more or less fixed over the short run.

As I explain in Chapter 9, depreciation is a unique expense. It is reported on a separate line in Exhibit 18.2. Accountants allocate a fixed amount of depreciation to each period, so it is reported as a fixed expense.

The classification of operating expenses requires careful study to sort out which costs belong in each of the expense categories. Once its operating costs have been classified this way, the costs are tagged in the bookkeeping process so that the total for each type of operating expense is determined and included in internal profit reports to managers.

Comparing Equal Percent Changes
in Sales Prices and Sales Volume

In the limited space of this chapter I can offer only a brief over-view of how business managers can use a profit report like the one shown in Exhibit 18.2. Speaking broadly, business managers focus on *changes*. Every factor and variable that determines profit is subject to change; change is constant, as experienced business managers will verify. In short, managers have to deal with changes that affect the profit performance of the business.

For example, higher transportation costs next year may increase the sales volume sensitive expenses. Property taxes may go up, which will increase fixed operating expenses. Or the sales manager may make a persuasive case that the advertising budget should be increased next year. Managers have to respond to all such changes; they don't get paid to sit on their hands and idly watch the changes happen.

Top-level managers have the responsibility of developing realistic plans to improve profit performance, which means making changes in the profit equation of the business. Which specific changes? This is the key question. Suppose the president of the company wants to develop a plan to improve bottom-line net income 10% next year. Exactly how would you accomplish this goal? The logical places to start are sales *prices* and sales *volume*.

Business managers need a crystal-clear understanding regarding what happens when sales prices increase (or decrease) and when sales volume increases (or decreases). Exhibit 18.3 compares the impacts of a 5% sales price increase scenario and a 5% sales volume increase scenario. In the sales price case, only sales prices change; all other profit factors remain the same for the year. In the sales volume case, only the quantities sold change; all other factors remain the same. In this comparison I stop at the earnings before interest and tax (EBIT) profit line. Generally, interest tends to follow sales revenue up and down, and income tax follows profit before income tax up and down—although I admit that these are very general comments.

Before looking at Exhibit 18.3, you might ask yourself which alternative you think is better. If you're a sales manager, you might favor the sales volume increase because the business would increase its market share at the higher sales volume. Market share is always an important factor to consider—I would never ignore this point. But, if you compare the two alternatives, you see that bumping the sales price 5% would be much better for profit.

Selling everything at 5% higher sales prices increases profit margin before fixed expenses 22.3% (see Exhibit 18.3), whereas selling 5% more of everything increases the profit margin before fixed expenses only 5%. Every variable expense goes up 5% with the 5% increase in sales volume. But only one expense goes up with the 5% sales price increase.

Then there are fixed selling and operating expenses and the fixed depreciation expense to consider. The higher sales prices

EXHIBIT 18.3—COMPARISON OF 5% SALES PRICE INCREASE VERSUS 5% SALES VOLUME INCREASE SCENARIOS

Dollar Amounts in Thousands

	Original Example	5% Higher Sales Prices			5% Higher Sales Volume		
		New Scenario	Change Amount	Change Percent	New Scenario	Change Amount	Change Percent
Sales Revenue	$ 52,000	$ 54,600	$2,600	5.0%	$54,600	$2,600	5.0%
Cost of Goods Sold Expense	(33,800)	(33,800)			(35,490)	(1,690)	5.0
Gross Margin	$ 18,200	$ 20,800	$2,600	14.3	$19,110	$ 910	5.0
Sales Revenue Sensitive Expenses	(4,420)	(4,641)	(221)	5.0	(4,641)	(221)	5.0
Sales Volume Sensitive Expenses	(3,120)	(3,120)			(3,276)	(156)	5.0
Profit Margin before Fixed Expenses	$ 10,660	$ 13,039	$2,379	22.3	$11,193	$ 533	5.0
Fixed Selling and Operating Expenses	(4,940)	(4,940)			(4,940)		
Fixed Depreciation Expense	(785)	(785)			(785)		
Earnings before Interest and Tax	$ 4,935	$ 7,314	$2,379	48.2%	$ 5,468	$ 533	10.8%

shouldn't affect fixed costs. However, a higher sales volume would push up some fixed costs if the business is already running at full capacity and would have to add more space, equipment, and personnel to handle the higher sales volume. In Exhibit 18.3 I assume that the business could take on 5% more sales volume without having to increase any of its fixed costs.

It may be more realistic, though, to gain 5% more sales volume compared with pushing through a 5% sales price increase. Customers may balk at the higher sales prices. Setting sales prices certainly is one of the most perplexing decisions facing business managers. The price sensitivity of customers is seldom clear-cut. In any case, business managers should understand that a relatively small change in sales price could have a major impact on profit margin.

The format of the management profit report presented in Exhibit 18.3 can be used as a *template* or *model* for analyzing, budgeting, and planning profit. For instance, the business may plan for a 10% sales volume increase combined with 5% sales price increases across the board next year. You can fairly easily make these changes and see what the profit (before interest and income tax expenses) would be if these changes hold true next year.

You can use the management profit report template (Exhibit 18.2) to determine the *breakeven point* at lower sales prices and lower sales volume. Exhibit 18.4 reveals that a 10.4% drop in sales prices would wipe out all the company's earnings before interest and income tax (EBIT). In contrast, sales volume would have to plunge 46.3% to take the business down to its EBIT breakeven point. (Using an Excel spreadsheet, I decreased sales price and sales volume to find the two breakeven points.)

Exhibit 18.4 makes clear that the business should be very careful regarding its sales prices. In particular, a 10% drop in sales prices would take the business very close to its breakeven point if volume stays the same. Its sales manager might suggest a cut in sales prices to boost sales volume, however. First, I'd recommend that you use the profit report template (Exhibit 18.2) to crunch the numbers, and see whether profit would increase.

EXHIBIT 18.4—EBIT BREAKEVEN POINT FOR LOWER SALES PRICES AND LOWER SALES VOLUME

Dollar Amounts in Thousands

	Original Example	Sales Price Decrease			Sales Volume Decrease		
		Breakeven Scenario	Change		Breakeven Scenario	Change	
			Amount	Percent		Amount	Percent
Sales Revenue	$ 52,000	$ 46,607	$(5,393)	−10.4%	$ 27,929	$(24,071)	−46.3%
Cost of Goods Sold Expense	(33,800)	(33,800)			(18,154)	15,646	−46.3
Gross Margin	$ 18,200	$ 12,807	$(5,393)	−29.6	$ 9,775	$ (8,425)	−46.3
Sales Revenue Sensitive Expenses	(4,420)	(3,962)	458	−10.4	(2,374)	2,046	−46.3
Sales Volume Sensitive Expenses	(3,120)	(3,120)			(1,676)	1,444	−46.3
Profit Margin before Fixed Expenses	$ 10,660	$ 5,725	$(4,935)	−46.3	$ 5,725	$ (4,935)	−46.3
Fixed Selling and Operating Expenses	(4,940)	(4,940)			(4,940)		
Fixed Depreciation Expense	(785)	(785)			(785)		
Earnings before Interest and Tax	$ 4,935	$ 0	$(4,935)	−100.0%	$ 0	$ (4,935)	−100.0%

Part Three

RELIABILITY OF FINANCIAL REPORTS

19

ACCOUNTING AND FINANCIAL REPORTING STANDARDS

Importance of Financial Reports

Millions of persons depend on financial reports for vital information about businesses. This sweeping congregation of financial report users includes bankers deciding whether to make loans to businesses; investors deciding whether to buy, hold, or sell stocks and debt securities of public corporations; buyers and sellers of private businesses deciding on the value of the company; owners of closely held businesses evaluating how their ventures are doing; suppliers deciding whether to sell to businesses on credit; and pension fund managers carrying out their fiduciary responsibility that requires due diligence in managing other people's money.

And let's not forget business managers themselves. Managers are the first and most immediate users of accounting information and financial statements. Managers depend on accounting reports to track their profit (or loss) performance. Managers need balance sheet and cash flow information to keep their financial condition under control, to spot any solvency problems that may be developing, and to plan for the capital requirements of the business. Managing the financial affairs of a business would be impossible without financial statements.

It goes without saying that financial statements and the accompanying disclosures should meet the information needs of users. Different readers focus on different information in financial reports. Financial statement users are generally interested in four basic financial aspects of a business:

1. Its sales *revenue* and *profit* (or loss) performance.

2. Its *financial condition* consisting of assets and liabilities, and in particular the *solvency* prospects of the company, which refers to the ability of the business to pay its liabilities on time and stay out of financial trouble.

3. Its *capitalization (ownership) structure*, which refers to the one or more classes of capital stock shares issued by the company, whether any debt of the company can be converted into capital stock, the number of stock options given to managers, and any other claims that directly or indirectly participate in the profit of the business.

4. Its *cash flow from profit-making (operating) activities* for the period, its cash distributions from profit to shareowners during the period, and its other sources and uses of cash flow during the period.

These four constitute the hard core of information that most investors and lenders look for in the financial statements and footnotes of a business.

This chapter discusses the standards that govern accounting methods and disclosure in financial reports by businesses. All *for-profit* business entities must abide by these rules of the game. (Not-for-profit organizations and governmental entities have their own accounting and financial reporting standards.) Imagine the confusion if each business were free to devise its own accounting methods, to invent its own financial terminology and financial statement formats, and to decide which additional information to disclose and which not to.

Investors, creditors, and others who read financial reports demand reasonably uniform and consistent standards that all businesses should follow in their financial reports. These standards are known as *generally accepted accounting principles* (GAAP) in the United States, and include both accounting methods and disclosure requirements.

For about 35 years now the center of power in the United States over financial reporting standards has been the *Financial Accounting Standards Board* (FASB). This highly qualified (and highly paid!) body is the top dog and primary authoritative source for financial reporting and accounting standards. The money for its operations comes from contributions from the accounting profession and businesses. It is a privately funded organization that does not have government support. Because of widespread financial reporting abuses and outright fraud in the early decades of the twentieth century, Congress passed important federal legislation governing the issuing and trading in securities as well as financial reporting by public companies.

The federal Securities and Exchange Commission (SEC) was created in 1934. It has broad jurisdiction over financial reporting by public companies in the United States. The SEC over the years has interceded occasionally where it decided that the FASB had failed to act, or when it took exception to the decisions of the FASB. However, by and large, the FASB (and its predecessors) have been the dominant source of financial reporting and accounting standards.

I believe the prevailing opinion is that, overall, the financial reporting system in the United States works well, and that GAAP is generally adequate for the purposes and functions of financial reporting. However, a rumble of criticism has persisted over the years. Perhaps expectations of financial statement users are too high and not entirely realistic. Financial accounting standards have a hard time keeping up with the rapid pace of changes in the business and economic environment.

In hindsight, one thing now is clear: Over the years the American accounting profession became chauvinistic. Until recently, the attitude of accountants in the United States was that our financial reporting and accounting standards were the best in the world. We became somewhat smug about this. We assumed that the rest of the world would catch up with our financial reporting and accounting standards. The creation of the European Union (EU), along with economic developments in the rest of the world, sent a clear signal that other countries would not simply fall in line with American financial reporting and accounting standards.

Moving Toward International Financial Reporting and Accounting Standards

Currently the main action in the world of accounting (and I do mean *world*) is the surprisingly quick pace toward the adoption of international financial reporting and accounting standards. In years past, each country had its own accounting rules—or lack of accounting rules. In 2001 the *International Accounting Standards Board* (IASB) was founded to establish global accounting principles. Its first order of business was to establish a comprehensive body of authoritative accounting and financial reporting standards for the EU member states.

The IASB quickly gained stature and broad support, and today has equal status with the FASB. It has issued many authoritative pronouncements on financial reporting and accounting standards, which are referred to as *international financial reporting standards* (IFRS). The June 2008 issue of *The CPA Letter*, the newsletter to American Institute of Certified Public Accountants (AICPA) members, mentions that more than 12,000 public companies in nearly 100 countries have adopted IFRS. Meanwhile, more than 10,000 public companies in the United States use GAAP. (Private companies in the United States also use GAAP, but see my comments about private companies later in the chapter.)

So, what we have at the present time (in 2008) are GAAP (generally accepted accounting principles) in the United States and IFRS (international financial reporting standards) outside the United States. Business, government, and accounting leaders quickly realized that a competition or war between GAAP and IFRS would cause all sorts of problems. No one was in favor of two sets of standards. Therefore, machinery was set up to move toward what is called the "harmonization" of GAAP and IFRS.

On the one hand, much progress has been made—there is a broad swath of agreement between GAAP and IFRS. On the other hand, some serious disagreements have not been resolved (at the time of revising this edition). Almost everyone thinks there is no choice but to move toward one set of international financial reporting and accounting standards. Recently the AICPA said that this should happen in five years or sooner.

Some long-accepted accounting methods in the United States may have to be abandoned or modified in order to conform to international standards. For instance, the international standards do not permit the use of the last-in, first-out (LIFO) method for recording cost of goods sold expense and inventory cost. Overall, though, we may end up with standards that are not too different from present GAAP, except that they will be called IFRS (international financial reporting standards).

One thing seems fairly certain: Most people think the setting of financial reporting and accounting standards should remain in the private sector and out of the hands of a government authority. How the role of the SEC and its counterpart agencies in other countries will evolve under international standards will be interesting to watch. The SEC has taken a strong leadership role in moving toward international standards; it has laid down a fairly aggressive timetable for public companies to implement international standards.

A Fly in the Ointment

One contentious issue between the FASB and IASB has emerged in moving toward the internationalization of financial reporting and accounting standards—the nature of the standards themselves. The IASB prefers the so-called *principles-based* approach, whereas the FASB uses the so-called *rules-based* approach. The differences between the two approaches are both philosophical and practical.

The principles-based IASB approach favors broadly stated standards that do not go into much detail and permit accountants in the field latitude in interpreting the standards. The thinking is that accountants have to consider a multitude of factors in real-life situations in complying with financial reporting and accounting standards. This approach recognizes that it is impossible to anticipate every conceivable set of circumstances in applying the standards. The idea is to make clear the spirit of the law and let accountants do the rest.

In stark contrast, the rules-based FASB approach issues standards that are written out in great detail and that attempt to have accountants comply with the letter of the law. Rules-based pronouncements seek to narrowly restrict the interpretation of standards and to keep the implementation of standards as close as possible to how the standards are written.

One serious problem with the rules-based FASB approach is that over the years the collection of authoritative pronouncements has become extremely complex and voluminous, and not internally consistent in all respects. Since its inception in 1973, the FASB has issued more than 160 official pronouncements. Assuming an average count of about 20 pages per standard, the FASB has issued thousands of pages of authoritative standards that accountants have to keep up with. The total count is probably over 5,000 pages if we include authoritative statements by the predecessors to the FASB, the SEC, other secondary sources of GAAP, and official interpretations of GAAP.

The FASB has recognized this problem. It is constructing an official condensed *codification* of GAAP, to provide a better road map for practicing accountants, academics, and others. It expects to release the codification in the near future. I can tell you that as an author I will definitely welcome a better-organized taxonomy of financial reporting and accounting standards.

Do Private Companies Need Separate Standards?

For years many accountants have had an intuitive feeling that the official statements by the FASB have been developed primarily for big companies whose stock and debt securities are traded in public markets—companies that are under the watch of government regulators. The concern is that the FASB standards are too onerous and are largely irrelevant to smaller privately owned businesses. Recently the FASB and the AICPA established an advisory Private Company Financial Reporting Committee to look into this issue and to make recommendations to the FASB.

Many GAAP pronouncements issued by the FASB over the years are not particularly relevant to most private businesses, and have thus had little impact on them. For instance, the standards on financial derivatives and management stock options don't apply to most small businesses. Also, the complex standards on business combinations and defined benefit retirement plans probably don't apply to most small private companies. However, certain FASB pronouncements dealing with disclosure in financial reports are stated in language that applies to both private and public companies. Did the FASB really mean that these disclosure requirements should apply to small mom-and-pop businesses?

The private company advisory committee has just gotten off the ground at the time of this writing. Frankly, I don't know what to expect from this committee. Private companies might consider leaving well enough alone, and not pressing for exemptions from some financial reporting standards. Few accountants would admit it, but in actual practice smaller private companies are not held to strict compliance with the official financial reporting and accounting standards. I'm not saying that private companies put out substandard financial reports that violate GAAP and that are seriously misleading. I simply mean that the implementation of GAAP by private companies is more relaxed, or however you prefer to put it.

The biggest differences between public and private companies are *not* in their basic accounting methods to measure revenue and expenses, and assets and liabilities. The main differences are in the extent of disclosure in their annual financial reports. Public companies disclose much more information in the footnotes to their financial statements and elsewhere in their annual financial reports. Private companies, in general, do not volunteer nearly as much information to their lenders and shareowners in their annual financial reports.

Stock Options

As you probably know, many public corporations grant *stock options* to their top-level executives. For example, suppose a company has issued 100 million shares of capital stock that are actively traded in a public stock market. Over the years it has granted several of its executives options to purchase stock shares at fixed prices equal to the market value of the stock at the time of granting the options. If all its options are eventually exercised, the company will have to issue 5 million additional shares. (Executives have to satisfy several conditions of employment before they have the right to exercise their options and buy the stock shares.)

Management stock options raise three basic accounting and financial reporting questions:

1. Should relevant details about the management stock options be *disclosed* so that the stockholders of the company and other readers of its financial reports are adequately informed about the stock options?

2. Should the number of potential stock shares that may be issued under terms of its management stock options be included in the calculation of the *diluted earnings per share* (EPS) of the company?

3. Should the company record an *expense* at the time of granting management stock options even if the exercise prices are equal to (or higher than) the market price of the stock shares?

Until recently the answers to these questions were yes, yes, and no. In other words, companies had to make adequate disclosure of their management stock options (usually in long and technical footnotes), and stock option shares were included in the calculation of diluted EPS. Initially this was the position of the FASB. Its thinking was that these two requirements were enough, and that stockholders could make their decisions accordingly.

Nevertheless, there was a loud outcry from several sources that companies, particularly those in the high-tech fields, were not reporting the full cost of their management compensation because they didn't recognize the expense of their management stock options. To repeat, companies had to disclose their management stock options and had to count the shares under these options in the calculation of their diluted EPS. But the chorus of dissent kept getting louder and louder.

Under intense pressure from many sides, the FASB revisited its pronouncement on stock options. To make a long story short, it revised its stance and adopted the position that at the time of granting management stock options an amount should be recorded as an expense—even when the exercise price of a stock option is equal to or higher than the market value of the stock. This expense does not have to be disclosed separately in the income statement. But the cost does have to be included somewhere in expenses in the income statement, with the result that net income is less.

Putting a value on a stock option at the time it is granted to an executive is rocket science. The valuation models for stock options are intensely mathematical. Companies can choose which particular valuation method they use. Not surprisingly, many companies select a method that minimizes the value put on their stock options, so that the expense is as small as possible.

Let me remind you here about expenses. Recording an expense decreases an asset or increases a liability. This basic point is taught in Accounting 101. However, recording stock option expense is a glaring exception to this fundamental concept of accounting. In recording the expense of a stock option, a business does *not* decrease an asset, nor does it increase a liability. So, how does a business record the expense for its stock options?

Well, the process of recording the expense for stock options may sound strange, but here goes. The business records an expense, which lowers net income and shareholders' equity. The amount of the stock option expense is also entered as an increase to shareholders' equity. Therefore, there is a wash effect on shareholders' equity. Why do such a thing?

Evidently the FASB was determined to get the expense on the books and run the expense through the income statement so that it affects net income. As you can tell from my remarks, I have serious reservations about the latest FASB pronouncement on management stock options. I think the FASB was right the first time, and should not have added the requirement to record an artificial expense for stock options.

The broader question is whether management stock options are necessary. Are stock options an effective management incentive? I share the view of Warren Buffett, the well-known investor and chairman and CEO of Berkshire Hathaway, who adamantly opposes stock options. The Berkshire Hathaway managers don't get stock options, but the businesses they run have done very well. Many critics argue that the financial gains from stock options realized by many executives are obscene and totally out of whack with their performance records.

In closing, I should mention that I have avoided technical details of accounting for stock options as an expense. I doubt you're very interested in these complex problems. I'll just say that there are very serious technical problems in measuring the cost of stock options. If nothing else, it can be said that stock options have caused a lot of problems in the business and financial worlds—beyond just accounting problems. To make their stock options more valuable, quite a few managers engaged in accounting fraud to overstate reported earnings of their companies.

Unfinished Business

The FASB should be given a lot of credit for dealing with several contentious accounting problems over the years. It has served as the authority for setting financial reporting and accounting standards. The FASB has also dealt with many industry-specific problems that needed attention, and it has issued many pronouncements on a variety of nagging accounting problems. However, I think it has fallen short in the general area of *income statement disclosure*.

For many years there have been persistent calls for more disclosure in financial reports. The central logic of the 1933 and 1934 federal securities laws is *full disclosure*. But several items of information—clearly of interest and relevance to investors, creditors, and other users of financial reports—don't have to be disclosed in external financial reports to shareowners.

Advertising and other marketing expenses do not have to be broken out separately in income statements, though they have to be reported in the annual 10-K filing with the Securities and Exchange Commission (SEC). Maintenance and repair expenses can be used to manipulate profit year to year (see Chapter 20). These expenses do not have to be reported in income statements, although they have to be disclosed in the annual 10-K with the SEC.

Compensation of top management does not have to be reported in a company's financial statements or in the footnotes. In contrast, this information must be disclosed in proxy statements of public corporations that are the means by which the boards of directors of corporations solicit the votes of stockholders.

A summary schedule of who owns the stock shares of a corporation does not have to be—and hardly ever is—disclosed in financial reports.

Disclosure has improved over the years, to be sure. For example, a regular feature in financial reports today is the *management discussion and analysis* (MD&A) section, which explains the profit performance, problems, and strategy of the business. In my opinion, disclosure could be expanded still further without causing businesses any loss of their competitive advantages.

To be fair about this, I should mention that most organizations—religious, military, educational, nonprofit, and governmental—are reluctant to make full disclosure of their financial affairs. Businesses are no exception to this general aversion to release too much information to the public.

Where do you get financial information about a company? Most public companies have web sites that include their financial reports and other information about the business. On their web sites the companies provide a direct link to the financial reports they file with the SEC. The SEC has an enormous database of filings by public companies under its jurisdiction. Go to www .sec.gov. This huge database of financial information is called the Electronic Data Gathering, Analysis, and Retrieval (EDGAR) system. In August 2008 the SEC announced the successor to EDGAR, which is called IDEA (interactive data electronic applications). IDEA will first supplement and then replace EDGAR.

20

ACCOUNTING METHODS AND MASSAGING THE NUMBERS

Chapter Preamble

The accounting methods used to record the activities of a business and to prepare its financial statements should conform to authoritative financial accounting standards. The shareowners and creditors who read the financial reports of a business are entitled to assume that its financial statements comply with established accounting standards, and that there are no serious violations of these standards. The primary purpose of audits of financial reports by an independent certified public accountant (CPA) is to ensure that proper accounting methods have been used by the business. (Chapter 21 discusses audits of financial reports.)

As you may have gathered from the chapter's title, the numbers reported in its financial statements depend on which *accounting methods* the business uses and whether the numbers have been massaged, or manipulated by its managers. For that matter, the financial statements may be fraudulent and provide bogus numbers for sales revenue and expenses. Or a business may discover later that financial statements it has issued have serious errors. In this latter situation, the business issues a *restatement* of its original financial statements in order to set the record straight, which I discuss at the end of the chapter.

Financial statements have the appearance of accuracy and finality, don't they? In financial statements you see a lot of numbers that are well organized and lined up in neat columns. But never lose sight of the fact that the numbers you see in financial statements depend on the accounting methods used to prepare the financial statements. If the recordkeeping process and accounting procedures of a business have errors (unintentional or deliberate), its financial statements have errors—maybe very serious errors.

In this chapter I encourage you to develop a healthy skepticism when reading financial statements. First, you should understand that the profit performance of the business and the values of its assets and liabilities depend on which particular accounting methods are chosen by the business. Second, you should understand that managers may take actions to affect the amounts of expenses and sales revenue for the year, in order to make profit come out closer to the number they want. Third, there's always a chance that the financial statements are fraudulent and seriously misleading. I don't want you to throw out the baby with the bathwater. But you should understand that some babies are given a bath in dirty water.

Now let me make one thing clear: I believe that the large majority of businesses have reliable recordkeeping systems and use honest, good-faith accounting methods. At the same time, the evidence is indisputable that some businesses do not exercise good faith in applying accounting methods and they deliberately issue heavily biased or outright fraudulent financial statements. My late father-in-law used to say, "There's a little bit of larceny in everyone's heart." Well, I might say that there's a lot of larceny in the hearts of those businesses that put out misleading financial statements.

Choosing Accounting Methods

In choosing its accounting methods, a business has to stay within the boundaries of *generally accepted accounting principles* (GAAP). These are the authoritative accounting standards in the United States, but see Chapter 19 regarding the movement toward international financial reporting standards. Don't think that GAAP puts a business in a straitjacket regarding its accounting methods. GAAP narrows down the range of choices but does not pin down a business to only one particular accounting method. In fact, for recording sales and many expenses a business can choose between alternative methods that are equally acceptable.

A business can adopt *conservative* accounting methods that delay the recording of profit, record lower values of certain assets, and record higher values of certain liabilities. Alternatively, a business can adopt *liberal* or *aggressive* accounting methods that have the reverse effects in its financial statements. Making decisions between liberal and conservative accounting methods is not a matter of choosing between good and bad accounting. Both conservative and liberal accounting methods are considered good accounting. Whether you vote Republican or Democratic doesn't mean you're a good or bad citizen.

Financial accounting would seem to be like measuring a person's weight on a scale that gives correct readings, wouldn't it? But, as a matter of fact, financial accounting standards permit a business to select which kind of scale to use—one that weighs light or one that weighs heavy.

This is not a textbook on accounting methods. All I can do here is give you a general idea of some areas in which a business can, quite legitimately, choose between alternative accounting methods:

- The exact timing for recording sales as complete and final, particularly when customers can return products, when there are significant post-sale expenses, and when sales prices are subject to later negotiation.

- When to record the expense of uncollectible accounts receivable from credit sales, and how to estimate the amount of these bad debts before they are actually written off at a future time.

- Whether to use first-in, first-out (FIFO), last-in, first-out (LIFO), or some other method for recording cost of goods sold expense and the cost value of inventory.

- Whether to use an accelerated (front-end loaded) depreciation method or the straight-line method, and whether to use short or longer (more realistic) useful life estimates.

- Whether to anticipate the likely loss in value of intangible assets or wait for clear evidence of the diminishment in value of intangible assets before recording the expense.

- Whether to immediately recognize future warranty and guarantee costs for products sold or wait until the work is done in later periods.

- Estimating the key variables that determine the cost of an employee-defined benefit retirement plan and a postretirement health/medical benefit plan.

This list is just a sampling of the decisions a business has to make for recording sales revenue and expenses. Of course, the net income for the period depends on the accounting methods selected by the business. In summary, a business has many accounting choices. Therefore, according to financial reporting standards it must disclose its significant accounting methods in the footnotes to its financial statements.

Most business managers probably welcome having a choice of accounting methods. In fact, they might prefer to have a broader range of choices for their accounting methods and for their financial report disclosures. The evolution of GAAP over the years has been in the direction of narrowing the range of acceptable accounting methods and expanding financial reporting disclosure requirements.

Note: A business does not have to disclose an estimate of the difference it would have made in its net income and in its asset and liability values if it had used alternative accounting methods.

A business doesn't have to go to the trouble of recomputing its sales revenue and all its expenses as if alternative accounting methods had been used instead of the accounting methods it actually uses. For example, a business does *not* say anything such as the following in its financial report:

> In the footnotes to the financial statements we explain that we use conservative accounting methods. If, instead, we had used liberal accounting methods, net income for the year just ended would have been $50 million higher, and assets and liabilities would have been significantly different than the amounts reported in the year-end balance sheet.

Finally, keep in mind that the choice of accounting methods does not affect cash flows during the year. The statement of cash flows (see Chapters 13 and 14) is the same regardless of which accounting methods are used. The statement of cash flows reports actual cash flows that occurred during the period. (However, a business may use a questionable technique called *window dressing* to improve its ending cash balance, which I discuss later in the chapter.)

Massaging the Numbers

During the year, business managers get regular profit reports from their accounting department. Toward the end of the year, and perhaps sooner, they should have a pretty good idea of the profit number that will be reported in the company's annual income statement. The projected profit may be significantly lower than they had forecast for the year (or much higher, for that matter). Broadly speaking, business managers have two courses of action in such a situation.

The managers could conduct business as usual. This means that they don't do anything special to deliberately affect the numbers that will be recorded for sales revenue and expenses in the year. (This does not preclude reducing costs where they can.) Or the managers could take action to cause net income for the year to come closer to what they want it to be. There are various steps managers can take to make net income behave, as it were.

In short, managers can do certain things for the main purpose of reducing or increasing expenses for the year (and sales revenue also). These management actions are generally called *massaging the numbers*. Managers put their thumbs on the scale, as it were, which has the effect of boosting or dampening the recorded profit for the year. As you would think, massaging the numbers raises ethical and moral questions, which unfortunately do not have easy and clear-cut answers.

Let me make clear the distinction between massaging the numbers and *cooking the books*. The latter term refers to *accounting fraud*, and fraud goes way beyond massaging the numbers.

Fraud involves falsifying sales revenue and expense amounts. Massaging the numbers refers to situations in which a business has recorded legitimate sales revenue and expenses, but managers take action to nudge the numbers up or down for the year. The best description of massaging the numbers I've heard was from my late father-in-law, a successful business owner/manager in his day. He said it was like "fluffing the pillows." I've always liked that characterization.

One can argue that massaging the numbers is not any worse than telling white lies, or embellishing the truth for the sake of a good story. Some say that massaging the numbers is like putting cosmetics on the financial face of the business (or like putting lipstick on a pig in some cases, I would say).

Most accountants are uncomfortable with it, but they understand that massaging the numbers is tolerated in the worlds of business and finance. (A Catholic might look upon massaging the numbers as a venial sin, but cooking the books would be a mortal sin.) Accountants would prefer that business managers not do it, but they go along with massaging the accounting numbers. You hardly ever hear an accountant blow the whistle on a business for massaging its numbers. Don't forget that the company's accountants are members of its management team.

One reason that managers massage their accounting numbers is to *smooth reported profit* year to year. Managers think that left on its own the accounting system generates net income numbers that behave too erratically, and that are too jerky year to year. They justify massaging the numbers on the grounds that they should "sand off the rough edges" of profit year to year. They argue that investors are better off because they don't overreact to year-to-year perturbations in reported net income and thereby do focus on the longer trend line of earnings.

Well, such reasoning for massaging the numbers is very difficult to judge. When a business has manipulated its accounting numbers for the year, it does not disclose what net income would have been without intervention by management. In any case, investors and creditors should realize that there's a good chance that the accounting numbers in the financial statements they are reading have been manipulated (massaged) to one degree or another.

Managers can massage the numbers in a variety of ways. For example, most businesses have *discretionary expenses*, which are those that depend heavily on the judgment of managers regarding how much to spend and when to make the expenditures. Consider repair and maintenance costs, for instance. Until the work is actually done, no expense is recorded. A manager can simply move back (or move up) the work orders for these expenditures. The building isn't painted this year, though it was scheduled to be. Or tires on delivery trucks are not replaced until next year, and so on. Using these tactics, a manager controls the amounts of some expenses that are recorded in the year.

Most businesses have many discretionary expenses. Two other discretionary expenses come to mind—employee training and development costs, and advertising expenditures. The manager in charge can delay sending employees on their normal schedule of training courses. An advertising campaign could be delayed until next year. The subsequent impacts of these actions on employee productivity and sales are difficult to assess, of course.

Another way in which managers can massage the accounting numbers involves the *end-of-year adjusting entries* that are recorded to bring certain expenses up to their full and complete balances for the year. Many of these year-end adjusting entries require estimates: the amount of accounts receivable that may not be collected in the future, the costs of future warranty work on products sold to customers, the rate of return that will be earned on the funds in the defined benefit employee retirement plan sponsored by the business, the decline in value of its intangible assets, and so on. Managers can lay a heavy hand on these estimates, thereby controlling the amount of expenses recorded in the year.

Managers can take certain actions to boost the amount of sales revenue recorded in the year. Sales can be accelerated, for example, by shipping more products to the company's captive dealers, even though they didn't order the products. This is called stuffing the channels of distribution. The business is taking away sales from next year to put the sales on the books this year. There are many other ways a business can give its sales for the year an artificial boost.

So far I have discussed massaging the numbers from the point of view of manipulating the amount of profit (net income) reported for the year. There is also a type of massaging the numbers that does not affect profit. Instead, the purpose is to make the short-term solvency and liquidity of the business look better than it really was at the end of the year. This practice is called *window dressing*.

Here's a common example of window dressing. A business holds open its books (its accounting records) for a few days after the end of its accounting year. The purpose is to record additional cash collections of accounts receivable. The cash collections are not actually received and in the hands of the company until the first few days in January 2010, for example, but the cash inflows are recorded as if they were collected December 31, 2009. The result is that its cash balance is higher and its accounts receivable is lower, which makes the company look more liquid (a larger cash balance). When I was in public accounting, we had clients who did this regularly. I suspect the same is true today, but I can't prove it.

One more time I should make clear that cooking the books goes beyond massaging the numbers. Cooking the books refers to recording sales revenue when in fact no sales were made, and not recording actual expenses or losses during the period. In short, cooking the books involves falsification of the accounting records. If massaging the numbers is carried too far, it can end up being equivalent to cooking the books (i.e., accounting fraud). In other words, massaging the numbers is a slippery slope that can lead to accounting fraud.

Business Managers and Their Accounting Methods

The chief executive officer (CEO) of a business has the responsibility that the company's financial statements are fairly presented, especially that the accounting methods used to measure the company's profit are within the range of methods permitted by established accounting standards. If its accounting methods are outside these limits, the company could stand accused of issuing false and misleading financial statements. The CEO would be liable for damages suffered by the company's creditors and stockholders who relied on its misleading financial statements. If for no other reason than this, the CEO should pay close attention to the choices of accounting methods used to prepare the company's financial statements.

Ideally, the chief executive of the business and its other top-level managers should decide which accounting methods and policies are best for the company. Of course the top-level managers should seek the advice of the company's chief financial officer and controller. They have to decide between conservative (cautious) versus liberal (aggressive) profit-accounting methods, which means whether to record profit later (cautious) or sooner (aggressive). The sooner sales revenue is recorded, the earlier profit is reported; and the later expenses are recorded, the earlier profit is reported.

If a business wants to report profit as soon as possible, the CEO should instruct the accountants to choose those accounting methods that accelerate sales revenue and delay expenses. In contrast, if the business wants to be conservative, it should order its accountants to use those accounting methods that delay the recording of sales revenue and accelerate the recording of expenses, so that profit is reported as late as possible. The accounting methods selected for cost of goods sold expense and depreciation expense are two key choices for businesses that sell products and invest heavily in long-term operating (fixed) assets.

Business managers may prefer to avoid getting involved in choosing accounting methods. I think this is a mistake. First, as already mentioned, there is the risk that the financial statements may not be prepared in complete accordance with GAAP, especially if an independent CPA does not audit the financial statements. Second, top-level managers should adopt those accounting methods that best fit the general policies and philosophy of the business. The CEO should decide which "look" of its financial statements is in the best interests of the business.

Somebody has to choose the accounting methods—if not its managers, then by default probably the company's controller. The controller, being the chief accounting officer of the company, should work hand in glove with the CEO and the other top-level managers to make sure that the accounting methods used by the business are not working at cross-purposes with the goals, objectives, strategies, and plans of the organization.

Consistency of Accounting Methods

Once a business chooses which accounting methods to use, the business sticks with these methods. A company does not flip-flop between accounting methods year to year. The Internal Revenue Service and the Securities and Exchange Commission take a dim view of switching accounting methods one year to the next. Furthermore, changing accounting methods causes a lot of disclosure problems in a business's financial statements and footnotes. Changes may be needed in certain circumstances, but the large majority of businesses don't switch their accounting methods except on rare occasions.

In short, consistency of accounting methods is the norm. Investors and lenders who read financial reports demand consistency of accounting methods year to year. Inconsistency would cause all sorts of problems in their year-to-year comparative analysis of a company's financial statements. It's tough enough as it is to analyze financial statements. Inconsistency of accounting methods would add another layer of difficulty. Financial accounting standards do not prohibit changing accounting methods, but a business should change methods only if there is sufficient reason to do so.

Quality of Earnings

You see the phrase *quality of earnings* in the business and financial press. Reported net income is put to a quality test, or litmus test as it were. The term does not have a precise definition, but clearly most persons who use this term refer to the integrity and trustworthiness of the accounting methods used by a business.

Conservative accounting methods are generally viewed as high quality. Stock analysts and professional investment managers view aggressive accounting methods with more caution. They like to see some margin for safety or some cushion for a rainy day in a company's accounting numbers. They know that many estimates and choices have to be made in financial accounting, and they would just as soon a business err on the low side in reporting profit rather than the high side.

Professional investors and investment managers are especially alert for accounting methods that appear to record revenue (or other sources of income) too early, or that fail to record losses or expenses that should be recognized. Even though the financial statements are audited, investment professionals go over them with a fine-tooth comb to get a better feel for how trustworthy the reported earnings of a business are.

They pay a lot of attention to cash flows from profit (operating activities) because this is one number managers cannot manipulate—the business either got the cash flow or it didn't. Accounting methods determine profit, but not cash flow. If reported profit is backed up with steady cash flow from operating activities (see Chapter 13), stock analysts rate the quality of earnings very high.

A basic principle of investing in stocks is to diversify your portfolio, so that investment risks are not too concentrated in just one stock or only a few stock holdings. One risk is that a company's financial report may be misleading, based on suspect accounting methods, or even fraudulent. Therefore, diversifying your stock holdings offers some protection against the risk of misleading and fraudulent financial reports.

Restatements of Financial Reports

Suppose you have just read an article in a newspaper. You assume that the facts in the article are correct, that it's reasonably complete and objective, and that the article is final. It's rather disconcerting when the newspaper later corrects some facts in the article or even runs a retraction of the article. You accepted the article as truthful and reliable, but then later the rug is pulled out from under you.

Well, you can imagine how readers of financial reports react when sometime later the company retracts the original financial report and puts out a revised version, which generally is called a *restatement* of the financial report. In almost all of these cases the new net income is considerably lower than the old net income that was first reported by the business.

While I was revising this book, a very interesting study was published about financial restatements: *The Changing Nature and Consequences of Public Company Financial Restatements, 1997–2006*, by Susan Scholz (U.S. Department of the Treasury, April 2008). Let me share with you a few of the study's findings (from the Executive Summary in the report).

Financial restatements are triggered by violations of U.S. generally accepted accounting principles (GAAP). The number of restatements exploded from only 90 in 1997 to 1,577 in 2006, and most of the large increase is accounted for by companies that do not trade on a major stock exchange. (So, you should be more careful about investing in these companies.) There was, as you would expect, a negative market reaction to the financial restatements, but the magnitude of the market decline leveled off starting in 2001. Fraud was a factor in 29% of all 1997 restatements, but only 2% of the 2006 restatements. Typically, restatements were by companies that were unprofitable before the restatement.

Although the study documents some troubling issues, I think a careful reading of the study's findings provides welcome reassurance that the financial statements issued by public companies are generally reliable and will not have to be restated at a later time. However, you can't be 100% certain about this, of course.

Last, I should mention that the financial statements of *private* companies have not been researched. There are, quite literally, more than a million private companies in the United States. Over the years I have seen quite a few financial statements of private companies. (I served on the board of directors of a local bank, for instance.) Generally, I have been disappointed with the financial statements of the private companies I've had the opportunity to read. I have to advise you to be a little more skeptical in reading the financial statements of a private company unless they have been audited by a CPA firm.

21

AUDITS OF FINANCIAL REPORTS IN THE POST-ENRON ERA

Opening Comments

Before getting into the discussion of audits of financial reports by independent certified public accountants (CPAs), I should open this chapter with a brief history of recent events. The Enron scandal was the tipping point that caused Congress and the public accounting profession to take action. During the last two decades of the twentieth century, an incredible number of accounting fraud cases were splashed across the headlines—WorldCom, Enron, Tyco, Ahold, Xerox, Rite Aid, Global Crossing, HealthSouth, Waste Management, and Adelphia Communications, to name just a few. Well-known and reputable CPA firms audited the financial statements of these companies.

When the financial reporting frauds committed by these companies became known, the market prices of their stock shares plunged and their shareholders suffered huge losses. Unfortunately, many employees of these companies had the bulk of their retirement savings invested in their own companies' stock shares. Many of these businesses went into bankruptcy. Frankly, I was astonished at the large number of accounting frauds. There had been accounting frauds over the years—in the 1930s and a rash in the 1960s. The accounting frauds in the 1980s and 1990s were much more troublesome.

Most of the companies that cooked their books were audited by the Big Five CPA firms, presumably the best auditors in the world. One CPA firm—Arthur Andersen—was convicted of obstruction of justice for destroying evidence in the Enron case. Almost overnight Arthur Andersen ceased to be. Thousands of its professional staff had to find jobs with other CPA firms or change their careers. The remaining Big Four CPA firms faced lawsuits and regulatory sanctions for failing to discover financial reporting fraud perpetrated by their audit clients.

The surge in the number and the large scale of accounting frauds caused Congress to pass the Sarbanes-Oxley Act of 2002 (SOX), which was signed into law by President George W. Bush. Many radical reforms were instituted by this piece of legislation, which I discuss in more detail later in the chapter. Auditors of public companies are now under the jurisdiction of a new federal regulatory agency. New responsibilities were imposed on corporate management and corporate audit committees.

In short, it's a new world for audits of financial reports of public companies—both for the CPA firms doing the audits and for the executives of the businesses being audited. The large majority of businesses that did not engage in accounting fraud are paying the price for the problems caused by the companies that did.

Why Audits?

Suppose you have invested a fair amount of money in a privately owned business. You are not involved in managing the company; you're an absentee owner—a passive investor. Being a stockholder, you receive the company's financial reports, of course. You read the financial statements and footnotes to keep informed about how the company is doing, and whether there might be any storm clouds on the horizon.

Let me ask you a question: How do you know whether the company's financial statements provide adequate disclosure and whether the business uses proper accounting methods to measure its profit? Do you just presume this? Are you sure you can trust the company's financial reports?

Or suppose you are a bank loan officer. A business includes its latest financial statements in its loan application package. Does the business use correct accounting methods to prepare its financial statements? Or have the financial statements perhaps been tweaked for purposes of securing the loan, to make them look better than they really are? It's not unheard-of, you know. (See Chapter 20 on massaging the numbers in financial statements.)

Or suppose you're a mutual fund investment manager in charge of a large portfolio of stocks traded on the New York Stock Exchange and Nasdaq. Market values of stock shares depend on the net income and earnings per share amounts reported by companies in their financial reports. How do you know that their profit numbers are reliable?

Financial statements can be seriously misleading for two reasons, one type being innocent in nature and the other type not so innocent:

1. **Honest Mistakes and Incompetency:** A company's internal accounting controls are inadequate and errors become imbedded in its accounting records, but the business fails to detect and correct the errors, or its chief accountant simply does not understand current accounting and financial reporting requirements and standards.

2. **Deliberate Dishonesty:** One (or more) of the top-level managers of a business intentionally distorts the company's profit performance and financial statements, or withholds vital information that should be disclosed in the financial report. This is called *financial reporting fraud* or *accounting fraud*. More popularly, it's called *cooking the books*.

One way to protect against the risks of errors and fraud is to *audit* the accounting system of the business to ascertain whether its financial statements are free of errors and adhere to appropriate accounting and financial reporting standards. An audit provides reassurance that the company's financial report is reliable and follows the rules. Audits of financial reports are done by independent *certified public accountants*, the profession we turn to next.

Certified Public Accountants

A person needs to do three things to become a certified public accountant (CPA). He or she must earn a college degree with a major in accounting with a fairly heavy emphasis in accounting courses. The American Institute of Certified Public Accountants (AICPA) has encouraged all states to enact laws requiring five years of education. Most but not quite all states have passed such laws.

Second, a person must pass the national CPA exam, which is a rigorous exam testing knowledge in accounting, income tax, auditing, and business law. Third, a person must satisfy the experience requirement of the state in which he or she lives. State laws and regulations differ regarding the time and nature of public accounting experience that a person must have; one year is generally the minimum.

After the three requirements are completed—education, exam, and experience—the person receives a license by his or her state of residence to practice as a CPA. No one else may hold himself or herself out to the public as a CPA. Most states (perhaps all, but I haven't checked this out) require 30 or 40 hours of continuing education a year to renew a person's CPA license. Every state has a Board of Accountancy that has the duty to regulate the practice of public accounting and the power to revoke or suspend the licenses of individuals who violate the laws, regulations, and ethics governing CPAs.

CPAs do more than just audit financial reports. They offer an ever-widening range of services to the public—income tax compliance and planning, personal financial consulting, business valuation, computer systems and information technology, production control and efficiency, forensic functions, and other fields of specialization. (*Note:* CPA firms that audit the financial reports of *public* companies are under tight restrictions regarding which particular nonaudit services they can provide to their audit clients.)

The CPA license is widely recognized and highly respected as a professional credential. The professional status of CPAs rests on their expertise and experience, and their independence from any one client. The word "certified" in their title refers to their expertise and experience. The term "public" refers to their independence. In doing audits of financial statements, the independence of the CPA is absolutely essential. To be independent, a CPA must be in public practice and not be an employee of any organization (other than the CPA firm itself, of course).

Public accounting experience is a good stepping-stone to other career opportunities. Many persons start in public accounting and end up as the controller (chief accountant), financial vice president, or chief financial officer (CFO) of an organization; some even become presidents and chief executive officers (CEOs) of business organizations. Some CPAs go into politics (a few have become state governors). Persons who have left public accounting are still referred to as CPAs even though they are not in public practice any longer. This is like a person with an M.D. degree who leaves the practice of medicine but is still called "doctor."

Are Audits Required?

Corporations whose debt and stock securities are traded publicly are required by federal securities laws to have their annual financial reports audited by an independent CPA firm. Most estimates put the number of public companies at about 10,000 in the United States. Private businesses are not covered by federal securities laws, but are subject to such state laws as apply to them. There are more than nine million for-profit business corporations, partnerships, and limited liability companies, as well as millions of sole proprietorships (one-owner business ventures). Although they are not *legally required* to have audits, many private business entities have their annual financial reports audited by a CPA firm.

I served on the board of directors (and was a stockholder) of a privately owned bank, and we had CPA audits every year. Lawyers should be consulted regarding state corporation and securities laws; an audit may be required in certain situations. A private business may sign a contract or agree informally to have its annual financial reports audited as a condition of borrowing money or when issuing capital stock to new investors in the business.

As just mentioned, public corporations have no choice; they are legally required to have audits of their annual financial reports by independent CPA firms. But, if not required, should a business hire a CPA firm to audit its annual financial report? What's the payoff? Basically, an audit adds *credibility* to the financial

report of a business. Audited financial reports have a higher "believability index" than unaudited statements.

Audits by CPAs help provide protection against misleading financial statements. CPA auditors are expert accounting detectives, and they thoroughly understand accounting and financial reporting standards. Being independent of a business, the CPA auditor should not tolerate a misleading financial report.

Audits don't come cheap. CPAs are professionals who command high fees. A business cannot ask for a "once-over lightly" audit at a cut rate. An audit is an audit. CPA auditors of private businesses are bound by *generally accepted auditing standards* (GAAS), and the auditors of public companies have to follow the regulations of the federal agency created by the Sarbanes-Oxley Act of 2002. Violations of auditing standards and regulations can result in lawsuits against the CPA, sanctions by the federal regulatory agency, and damage to the CPA's professional reputation, of course.

An audit takes a lot of time, because the CPA has to examine a great deal of evidence and make many tests of the accounting records of the business before being able to express an opinion on the company's financial statements. The time it takes to complete an audit causes the relatively high cost of the audit. A business, assuming an audit is not legally required, has to ask whether the gain in credibility of its financial report is worth the cost of the audit.

A bank may insist on an audit as a condition of making a loan to a business. The outside (nonmanagement) stockholders of a business may insist on annual audits to protect their investments in the business. In these situations, the audit fee can be viewed as a cost of using external capital. In many situations, however, outside investors and creditors do not insist on audits. Even so, a business may choose to have an audit as a checkup on its accounting system. Or a business may decide it needs to have a security check—an independent examination focusing on whether the business is vulnerable to fraud and embezzlement schemes.

When they hear the word "audit," most people think of discovering wrongdoing and ferreting out dishonesty. But this is *not* the primary purpose of an audit of a financial report by an independent CPA. In the course of doing the audit, the CPA may discover embezzlement by employees, or may uncover high-level accounting fraud. However, the primary purpose of an audit of a financial report by a CPA is to attest to the *fairness* of the financial statements and disclosures in the financial report of the business. Fairness means, primarily, conformity of the company's accounting methods and disclosures with established accounting and financial reporting standards.

The purpose of a financial report audit by a CPA is like the reason an individual has a general physical exam once a year. The physician performs standard tests and evaluates your overall condition, and at the same time should be alert for any trouble signs out of the ordinary. Unless there is some reason to look for cancer or heart problems, the doctor does not do extensive examinations for these problems. For instance, the doctor doesn't order an X-ray unless he or she suspects a problem that requires this additional procedure.

CPA auditors are required to plan their audit procedures to search for possible accounting fraud and to identify weak internal controls that would allow such fraud to go undetected. Nevertheless, the main purpose of an audit is to express an opinion on the fairness of financial statements (including footnotes), and whether the financial statements adhere to generally accepted accounting principles (in the United States).

Fraud would undermine the integrity of the financial statements, of course, so the CPA auditor has to be on the lookout for fraud of all types (as well as for accounting errors). But the CPA says nothing at all about fraud in the audit report. There is no statement such as "We looked for fraud but didn't find any." What the CPA auditor does say is discussed next.

Clean Audit Opinion

First of all, let's be clear on one point. I'm talking specifically about *audits of business financial reports by CPAs*. There are many other kinds of audits, such as an audit of your income tax return by the Internal Revenue Service (IRS), audits of federally supported programs by the Government Accountability Office (GAO), audits by the internal auditors of an organization, and so on. The following discussion concerns audits by CPAs of financial reports prepared by businesses that are released to the outside world—primarily to their lenders, shareholders, and others who have a legitimate right to receive a copy of the financial report.

Financial report readers are not too concerned about how an audit is done, nor should they be. The bottom line to them is the opinion of the CPA auditor. They should read the opinion carefully, although there is evidence that most don't or at best just give it a quick glance. Evidently many financial report readers simply assume that having the financial report audited is, by itself, an adequate safeguard. They assume that the CPA would not be associated with a financial report that is incorrect or misleading.

Many financial report readers seem to think that if the CPA firm gives an opinion and thereby is associated with a financial report, then the financial statements and footnotes must be okay and are not wrong in any significant respect. Doesn't the CPA's opinion constitute a stamp of approval? No, not necessarily!

The best audit opinion is called an *unqualified opinion*, or more popularly a "clean" opinion. The standard three-paragraph language of a clean opinion recommended by the Auditing Standards Board of the AICPA is presented in Exhibit 21.1.

Basically this unqualified, or clean, opinion states that the CPA has no significant disagreements with the financial statements and disclosures of the company. Putting this differently, the CPA *attests* that the financial statements have been prepared according to generally accepted accounting principles (GAAP) in the United States and that the footnotes plus other information in the financial report provide adequate disclosure. (These standards leave management a range of choices of accounting methods, which I discuss in Chapter 20.)

In a clean opinion, the CPA auditor says, in effect, "I don't disagree with the financial report." The CPA, if he or she were the controller of the business, might have prepared the financial statements differently and might have written the footnotes differently. In fact, the CPA auditor might prefer that different accounting methods had been used. What the CPA expresses in a clean opinion is that the company's financial statements and disclosures do not in any material manner violate established accounting and financial reporting standards.

The auditing profession thought that it should be made clear that an audit provides reasonable but not absolute assurance that "the financial statements are free of material misstatement." And it was thought that users of financial reports should be told briefly what an audit involves (see the second paragraph).

The standard version of the CPA auditor's report runs 209 words of fairly technical jargon, and in my opinion demands a lot from the reader. Be honest: Did you carefully read every sentence in the standard audit report in Exhibit 21.1? I'd bet that you only skimmed each paragraph.

In the standard audit report you should take notice of the words "An audit includes examining, *on a test basis...*" The auditor does not examine every transaction of a business during the year and does not examine every item making up the total balance of specific assets and liabilities. In a word, auditors rely on *sampling*. CPA auditors, therefore, pay particular attention to the *internal controls* of the company that are designed to deter and detect errors and irregularities. CPA auditors are required to carry out *risk assessment procedures*, to identify the likely areas of errors and irregularities and to concentrate their audit procedures in the high-risk areas.

The cost of making all audits absolutely fail-safe would be prohibitive. In the grand scheme of things, a few audit failures are tolerated in order to keep the overall cost of audits within reason. In moments of deep cynicism, it has occurred to me that perhaps the real reason for audits is to provide business lenders and investors someone to sue when they suffer losses and there is evidence that the company's financial reports were misleading or fraudulent.

EXHIBIT 21.1—STANDARD UNQUALIFIED OR CLEAN AUDITOR'S REPORT

Independent Auditor's Report

We have audited the accompanying balance sheets of X Company as of December 31, 20X2 and 20X1, and the related statements of income, retained earnings, and cash flows for the years then ended. These financial statements are the responsibility of the Company's management. Our responsibility is to express an opinion on these financial statements based on our audits.

We conducted our audits in accordance with auditing standards generally accepted in the United States of America. Those standards require that we plan and perform the audit to obtain reasonable assurance about whether the financial statements are free of material misstatement. An audit includes examining, on a test basis, evidence supporting the amounts and disclosures in the financial statements. An audit also includes assessing the accounting principles used and significant estimates made by management, as well as evaluating the overall financial statement presentation. We believe that our audits provide a reasonable basis for our opinion.

In our opinion, the financial statements referred to above present fairly, in all material respects, the financial position of X Company as of [at] December 31, 20X2 and 20X1, and the results of its operations and its cash flows for the years then ended in conformity with accounting principles generally accepted in the United States of America.

[*Signature*]

[*Date*]

Do Auditors Discover Accounting Fraud?

In Chapter 20 I distinguish between *massaging the numbers* and *accounting fraud*. Massaging the numbers involves nudging accounting numbers one way or the other. Business managers take actions to control the amounts of sales revenue and expenses recorded in the period, in order to smooth profit year to year or to give profit a temporary boost up (or a push down). Such accounting tactics are in a gray area of accounting ethics. CPA auditors certainly don't like to discover these management machinations regarding the accounting numbers. However, manipulating the accounting numbers is tolerated in the business world—as long as it doesn't go too far so as to cause seriously misleading financial statements.

Massaging the numbers can be likened to a misdemeanor. In this vein, accounting fraud is a felony. Cooking the books goes way beyond nudging the numbers up or down a little. Accounting fraud involves falsification or fabrication of sales revenue and expenses, and reporting assets that don't exist or not reporting liabilities that do exist. In short, accounting fraud creates financial statements that are deliberately misleading—and seriously so.

Do CPA auditors always discover accounting fraud? The short answer is: not necessarily. CPA auditors *may* discover accounting fraud. However, if the managers who commit fraud cleverly conceal the fraud and if their schemes are well thought out, accounting fraud can go undiscovered for years. Having an audit by an independent CPA certainly increases the chances of uncovering accounting fraud, but does not guarantee that fraud will be uncovered in every instance.

What it comes down to, in my view, is that the cost of an audit has to be kept under control. The audit cost has to be reasonable relative to the benefits of the audit. Given the cost constraint on an audit, the CPA cannot search and test for every conceivable fraud that could be going on in the business. The CPA auditor should evaluate the controls established by the business to guard against financial reporting fraud. If the auditor discovers weaknesses in these controls, the auditor should investigate the vulnerable areas and work closely with the company's audit committee to remedy the weaknesses.

At the end of the day, there's always some risk that the CPA auditor may not discover accounting fraud—especially if the top-level managers of the business instigate the fraud.

Reading the Auditor's Report

The vast majority of financial report readers, in my opinion, simply want to know whether the CPA has any objection to the financial statements and footnotes prepared by management. They don't care that much about the specific wording used in the CPA auditor's report. They want to know one main thing: Does the CPA auditor give his or her blessing to management's financial report? If not, they want the CPA auditor to make clear his or her objections to the financial report.

Financial report users should read the CPA auditor's report to see first, whether the auditor gives a clean opinion, and second, whether the auditor provides any additional information that might constitute something less than a clean opinion. The standard three-paragraph audit report is expanded in the following situations:

- The CPA auditor wants to emphasize one or more points, such as related-party transactions reported in the financial statements, significant events during the year, or unusual uncertainties facing the business.

- The company has changed its accounting methods between the most recent year and previous years, which causes inconsistencies with the originally issued financial reports of the business.

- There is substantial doubt about the entity's ability to continue as a going concern, because of financial difficulties in meeting the due dates for payment of its liabilities, or because of other large liabilities it is not able to pay.

Such additional information in the audit report does not constitute a qualification on the company's financial report; it just provides more information.

In contrast, the CPA auditor may take exception to an accounting method used by the company, or to the lack of disclosure for some item that the CPA thinks is necessary for adequate disclosure. In this situation, the CPA renders a *qualified opinion* that includes the key words "except for" in the opinion paragraph. The grounds for the qualification (what the auditor takes exception to) are explained in the auditor's report. To give a qualified opinion, the CPA auditor must be satisfied that, taken as a whole, the financial statements and footnotes are not misleading.

A qualified opinion may be due to a limitation on the scope of the CPA's examination. The CPA is not able to gather sufficient evidence for one or more accounts in the financial statements, and therefore has to qualify or restrict his or her opinion with regard to these items.

How serious a matter is a qualified opinion? The auditor points out a flaw in the company's financial report, but not a fatal flaw. A qualified audit opinion is a yellow flag, but not a red flag. Keep one thing in mind: The CPA auditor must judge that the overall fairness of the financial report is satisfactory, even though there are one or more deviations from established accounting and disclosure standards. If the auditor is of the opinion that the deviations are so serious as to make the financial statements misleading, then the CPA must issue an *adverse opinion*. You hardly ever see an adverse opinion. No business wants to put out misleading financial statements and have the CPA auditor say so for everyone to see!

The CPA auditor may have to *disclaim an opinion* due to limitations on the scope of the audit or due to very unusual uncertainties facing the business. In some situations a CPA may have very serious disagreements with the client that cannot be resolved to the auditor's satisfaction. The CPA may withdraw from the engagement (i.e., walk off the audit). This is not very common, but it happens every now and then. In these situations the CPA has to notify top management, the board of directors of the company, and its audit committee, and make clear the nature of the disagreements and why the CPA is withdrawing from the audit.

The CPA does not act as a whistle-blower beyond the inner confines of the company. For public companies, the CPA has to inform the SEC that the firm has withdrawn from the audit engagement and whether there were any unresolved disagreements between the CPA and the company. Also, the CPA auditor should work closely with the audit committee of a public company, and is duty-bound to communicate to the committee issues that come up in the course of the audit.

Post-SOX

As I mention at the start of the chapter, Congress passed the Sarbanes-Oxley Act of 2002 (SOX) in response to many well-publicized audit failures, culminating in the infamous Enron fiasco. This important piece of federal legislation is designed to improve the quality of audits and the independence of CPA auditors. Congress was upset with the fact that auditors failed to discover enormous accounting frauds that happened under their very noses. Congress was in no mood to hear any more excuses and promises from the auditing profession.

The act created a new federal agency called the *Public Company Accounting Oversight Board* (PCAOB), which is a branch of the Securities and Exchange Commission (SEC). The PCAOB has enormous power over the CPA firms that audit public companies. It might have been better to call the board the "Public Company *Auditing* Oversight Board." The PCAOB is given broad powers and has the dominant role in regulating the auditing of public companies.

The Sarbanes-Oxley Act also imposes new financial reporting duties on corporate management. The CEO has to certify that his or her company's financial report is presented fairly and is in full compliance with all relevant accounting and financial reporting standards. Also, management is required to state its opinion on the internal controls of the business in the annual financial reports.

The CPA auditing profession is now split into two segments: audits of *public* companies and audits of *private* companies. The Auditing Standards Board of the AICPA issues authoritative auditing pronouncements that govern audits of private companies. The PCAOB controls the rules for auditing public companies, although areas in which the agency has not taken action are still governed by the standards of the AICPA's Auditing Standards Board.

Although the initial costs of implementing the several requirements of SOX were high, subsequent developments have shown that the costs have leveled off and even gone down somewhat. The general opinion seems to be that the quality of audits has improved.

Another outcome of SOX is that audit committees of companies now have more authority and responsibility for the financial reports of their companies. I know that if I were now asked to serve on the audit committee of a public company I would think long and hard about it. I happen to know a person who was on Enron's audit committee. I wouldn't want to be in his shoes.

22

PARTING COMMENTS

Some years ago a women's investment club invited me to their monthly meeting to explain financial statements. It was a lot of fun. These women are a savvy group of investors who pool their monthly contributions and invest mainly in common stocks traded on the New York Stock Exchange. Several of their questions were incisive, although one point caught me quite by surprise.

At that time they were thinking of buying common stock shares of General Electric (GE). Two members presented their research on the company with the recommendation to buy the stock at the going market price. The discussion caused me to suspect that several of the members thought their money would go to GE. I pointed out that the money would go to the seller of the stock shares, not to GE.

They were not entirely clear on the difference between the *primary* capital market (the original issue of securities by corporations for money that flows directly into their coffers), and the *secondary* securities trading market (in which people sell securities they already own to other investors, with no money going to the companies that originally issued the securities). I compared this with the purchase of a new car in which money goes to General Motors, Ford, or Honda (passing through the dealer) versus the purchase of a used car in which the money goes to the previous owner.

We cleared up that point, although I think they were disappointed that GE would not get their money. Once I pointed out the distinction between the two capital markets, they realized that whereas they were of the opinion that the going market value was a good price to buy at, the person on the other side of the trade must think it was a good price to sell at.

These women investors asked very thoughtful questions. I'd like to share these with you in this chapter, and answer a couple of other questions that are important for anyone who invests in stock and debt securities issued by public corporations, or who has an investment in a private business. Other financial statement readers should also find this chapter helpful.

Basic Questions and Answers

Business investors and lenders should know the answers to certain questions concerning financial statements. I answer these questions from the viewpoint of a typical individual investor, not an institutional investor or a professional investment manager. My retirement fund (TIAA-CREF) manages over $400 billion of investments. I assume its portfolio managers know the answers to these questions. They'd better!

Are financial reports reliable and trustworthy?

Yes, the vast majority of financial reports by *public* companies are presented fairly according to established standards, which are called generally accepted accounting principles (GAAP) in the United States and international financial reporting standards (IFRS) outside the United States. If not, the company's CPA auditor calls deviations or shortcomings to your attention. So, be sure to read the CPA auditor's report. At the time of revising the book, American and international accounting and financial reporting standards were in the process of being merged into one coherent body of standards. How this "harmonization" process will end up is hard to predict.

The financial reports of *private* companies that are audited by CPAs are as generally reliable as those of public companies. (At least this has been my experience.) However, *unaudited* financial reports of private companies are more at risk of violating one or more accounting and financial reporting standards. For example, I have seen private company financial reports that did not include a statement of cash flows, even though this financial statement was required at the time. Much depends on the competence of the chief accountant of the business. When reading unaudited financial statements of smaller private companies, you should be more on guard.

You should realize that accounting and financial reporting standards are not static. The rule-making authorities constantly monitor financial reporting practices and emerging problem areas. They make changes when needed, especially to keep abreast of changes in business and financial practices, as well as developments in the broader political, legal, and economic environments in which businesses live and operate.

Nevertheless, are some financial statements misleading and fraudulent?

Yes, unfortunately. The *Wall Street Journal* and the *New York Times* carry stories of accounting fraud instigated by high-level managers in businesses. These financial report shenanigans are done in various ways. Sales revenue can be overstated or expenses and losses are understated or not recorded at all. Net income is inflated in order to prop up the market price of the stock shares. Or a business may not disclose serious problems in its financial condition. In committing accounting fraud, the business lies to its lenders and shareowners. The company deliberately misleads its stakeholders by reporting false financial information, and the managers know that it is false.

It is difficult for CPA auditors to detect accounting fraud that is initiated and "sponsored" by high-level managers, especially if it is cleverly concealed and involves conspiracy among managers and other parties to the fraud. (Chapter 21 discusses financial statement audits by CPAs.) Auditors are highly skilled professionals, and the failure rate of auditors to discover fraud has been relatively low. However, in some cases CPAs were negligent in carrying out their audits and deserved to be sued—and they were!

The bottom line is that there is a small risk that the financial statements you depend on are, in fact, false and seriously misleading. You would have legal recourse against the company's executives and its auditors once the fraud is found out, but this is not a happy situation. Almost certainly you'd end up losing money, even after recovering some of your losses through legal action.

Is it worth your time to compute financial statement ratios?

I doubt it. Even though the conventional wisdom is that by diligent reading of financial statements you will discover under- or overvalued securities, the evidence doesn't support this premise. Market prices reflect all publicly available information about a business, including the information in its latest quarterly and annual financial reports. (Insiders may be privy to information about coming events and take advantage of their position to make trades before the information becomes public knowledge.)

Computing financial statement ratios can be a valuable learning experience. But don't expect to find out something that the market doesn't already know. It's very unlikely that you will find a nugget of information that has been overlooked by everyone else. Forget it; it's not worth your time as an investor. The same time would be better spent keeping up with current business and economic developments reported in the financial press.

Why read financial statements, then, if you won't find information that has been overlooked by others?

You want to know what you are getting into. Does the company have a lot of debt and a heavy interest load to carry? For that matter, is the company in bankruptcy or in a debt workout situation? Has the company had a consistent earnings record over the past 5 to 10 years, or has its profit ridden a roller coaster over this time? Has the company consistently paid cash dividends for many years? Has the company suffered a major loss recently? Has the company given its executives stock options on a large number of shares? Has the company issued more than one class of stock shares?

You would obviously inspect a house before getting serious about buying it, to see if it is in good condition and whether it has two stories, three or more bedrooms, a basement, a good general appearance, and so on. Likewise, you should know the "financial architecture" of a business before investing your capital in its securities. Financial statements serve this getting-acquainted purpose very well, as long as you know what to look for.

One basic stock investment strategy is to search through financial reports or financial statement data on web sites, to find corporations that meet certain filtering criteria—for example, whose market values are less than their book values or whose cash and cash equivalent per share are more than a certain percent of their current market value. Whether these stocks end up beating the market is another matter. In any case, financial statements can be culled through to find whatever types of companies you are looking for.

The financial statements and footnotes of large public companies would take several hours to read carefully. What's the alternative?

Large businesses produce large financial reports! Their financial statements generally are long, complex, and include several pages of densely written footnotes. Quite literally it would take you several hours, or even longer, to conscientiously read every item in every financial statement of a company, and every sentence in every footnote. Also, don't forget the auditor's report (also written in technical language), the letter from the CEO to shareholders, and the statement by top management concerning its responsibility for internal controls designed to prevent fraudulent financial reporting. I have to wonder whether professional stock analysts and investment managers have the time to read through the entire financial reports of all the companies they follow and invest in. Maybe they delegate this job to their subordinates, in which case I hope *they* have the time and understand financial statements.

Being aware of how long it takes to read their financial reports cover to cover, most public companies provide *condensed annual financial statements* to their shareholders. The actual financial statements of the business are collapsed into brief summaries of their income statement, balance sheet, and statement of cash flows. These condensed financial statements are *not* accompanied by footnotes and often do not refer to the CPA auditor's report.

If you don't have time to delve into the actual financial statements and footnotes of a company, you should at least read its condensed financial statements. This is better than nothing. By the way, most not-for-profit organizations (such as AARP, for example) issue condensed financial statements to their members. So does my retirement fund manager, TIAA-CREF. I still ask for its actual financial statements. As I start reading them I know I'm in for a long night that only an accounting professor could love.

Is there any one basic litmus test for a quick gauge of a company's financial performance?

I suggest that you compute the percent increase (or decrease) in sales revenue this year compared with last year, and use this percent as the baseline for testing changes in bottom-line profit (net income) as well as the changes in the major operating assets of the business. Assume sales revenue increased 10% over last year. Did profit increase 10%? Did accounts receivable, inventory, and long-term operating assets increase 10%?

This is no more than a quick-and-dirty method, but it will point out major disparities. For instance, suppose inventory jumped 50% even though sales revenue increased only 10%. This may signal a major management mistake; the overstock of inventory might lead to write-downs later. Management does not usually comment on such disparities in financial reports. You'll have to find them yourself.

Do financial statements report the truth, the whole truth, and nothing but the truth?

There are really two questions here. One question concerns how truthful is profit accounting, which depends on the company's choice of accounting methods from the menu of generally accepted alternatives and how faithfully the methods are applied year in and year out. The other question concerns how honest and forthright the disclosures in the company's financial report are.

Revenue and expenses should be recorded faithfully and honestly according to the accounting methods adopted by the business. In other words, once accounting choices have been made, the business should apply the methods and let the chips fall where they may. However, there is convincing evidence that managers of public companies occasionally, if not regularly, intervene and take certain actions to affect the amounts recorded in sales revenue and expenses to produce more favorable results than would otherwise happen—something akin to the "thumb on the scale" trick. (I discuss massaging the numbers in Chapter 20.)

Manipulating the accounting numbers is done to smooth reported earnings, or to balance out unwanted perturbations and oscillations in annual earnings. Investors in public companies seem to prefer a nice steady trend of earnings instead of unpredictable fluctuations, and managers oblige. So, be warned that annual earnings probably are smoothed to some extent.

Disclosure in financial reports is another matter. Both public and private companies are generally reluctant to lay bare all the facts of interest to their lenders and shareholders. Bad news is usually suppressed or at least deemphasized as long as possible. Clearly, there is a lack of candor and frank discussion in many financial reports. Few companies are willing to wash their dirty linen in public by making full disclosure of their mistakes and difficulties in their financial reports.

Public companies include a *management discussion and analysis* (MD&A) section in their annual financial reports. But usually this is a fairly sanitized version of what happened during the year. The history of financial reporting disclosure practices, unfortunately, makes clear that until standard-setting authorities force specific disclosure standards on all companies, few will make such disclosures voluntarily.

Some years ago the disclosure of employee pension and retirement costs went through this pattern of inadequate reporting until, finally, the standard-setting body in the United States stepped in and required fuller disclosure. Recalls of unsafe products, pending lawsuits, and top management compensation are examples of reluctant reporting. Here is a historical example: Until the standard was adopted in 1987, companies did not report a statement of cash flows, even though this information had been asked for by security analysts since the 1950s!

The masthead of the *New York Times* boasts "All the News That's Fit to Print." Don't expect this in companies' financial reports, however.

Does its financial report explain the basic profit-making strategy of the business?

Not really. In an ideal world, I would argue, a financial report should not merely report how much profit (net income) was earned by the business and the amounts of revenue and expenses that generated this profit. The financial report should also provide a profit road map, or an earnings blueprint of the business. Financial report readers should be told the basic profit-making strategy of the business, including its most critical profit-making success factors.

In their annual financial reports, publicly owned corporations are required to disclose their sales revenue and operating expenses by major segments (lines of business). Segmenting a business into its major lines of sales provides information about which major product lines are more profitable than others. However, segments are conglomerate totals that span many different products. Segment disclosure was certainly a step in the right direction. For example, the breakdown between domestic versus international sales revenue and operating profit is very important for many businesses.

Businesses are very careful not to divulge too much information in their financial reports about their profit margins on specific products (and services). For example, Apple does not reveal how much money it makes on sales of its iPhone versus its iMac, and so on. Profit margin information is treated as very confidential, and is kept away from competitors and from investors in the business as well. The income statement in an external financial report is not the profit report you would see if you were the CEO of the business.

Does the market price of a public company's stock shares depend directly and only on the information reported in its financial statements?

Well, you know the answer to this question, don't you? The market price of a public company's stock shares depends on many factors, although the information reported in its financial statements is the main point of reference. I include this question only to remind you that a public company's financial statements are only one source—albeit one of the most important sources—of the information that investors use to make their buy, hold, and sell decisions.

Does the balance sheet of a private business tell the market value of the business?

No. The balance sheet of a private business does not report what the market value of the company would be if the business as a whole were on the auction block. The dollar amounts you see in a balance sheet are the results of its actual transactions and operations. The net income (bottom-line profit) reported in the annual income statement of a business summarizes its actual sales revenue for the year minus its actual expenses for the period. Likewise, the cash flows reported by the business are the actual amounts of cash flowing through the business during the year. In short, financial statements are prepared on a "look-back" or historical basis, not on a "look-ahead" basis for determining the market value of the business.

Until there is a serious buyer, it's anyone's guess how much a private business is worth. A buyer may be willing to pay much more than the book value of its owners' equity that is reported in its most recent balance sheet. The market value depends on many factors, as you probably know. Even Warren Buffett, the sage investor who is CEO of Berkshire Hathaway, admits that he has made mistakes in amounts he paid for some businesses, such as the Dexter Shoe Company (as told in his 2007 letter to stockholders, which you can read on the company's web site).

Generally, the market value of a private business depends mainly on its profit-making ability projected into the future. A buyer may be willing to pay 10 times the annual net income of a privately held business. But I would quickly add that other factors could also play a dominant role in setting the market value of a private business.

Also, I should mention that earnings-based values are quite different from liquidation-based values for a business. Suppose a company is in bankruptcy proceedings or in a troubled debt workout situation. In this unhappy position, the claims of its debt securities and other liabilities dominate the value of its stock shares and owners' equity. Indeed, the company's stock shares may have zero value in such cases.

Do books on investing and personal finance refer to financial statements?

It may come as a surprise to you, but generally these books say little to nothing about financial statements. The books make little effort to explain even the basics of financial statements, or ignore financial statements altogether. Don't get me wrong. There are many excellent books on investing and personal finance, and I have read quite a few of them.

I would warn you that some of the most popular of these books contain very little practical advice that you can actually use. Some of these books explain, for example, that if you save 10% of your annual income and invest it wisely, then after 40 years you will have a nice sum of money. As my grandkids would say: duh! In any case, I am perplexed that so few of the good investing and personal finance books discuss financial statements in any depth, or they ignore financial statements altogether.

Financial statements are the essential wellspring of information for business investors and lenders. Indeed, where else do you get this vital information? Not having this financial information would be like trying to find your destination in a city without street signs and traffic signals.

A Very Short Summary

You can generally rely on audited financial statements, although the rash of accounting frauds during the 1980s and 1990s that CPA auditors failed to discover shook my confidence somewhat. Overall, the percent of fraudulent financial reports among all public businesses is very low. In any case, investors don't really have an alternative source of financial information about a business other than its financial statements. Accounting fraud, unfortunately, is an unavoidable risk of investing.

You might think twice before investing much time in analyzing the financial statements of corporations whose securities are publicly traded—because thousands of other investors have done the same analysis and the chance of you finding out something that no one else has yet discovered is virtually nil. For a quick benchmark test, though, you might compare the percent change in the company's sales revenue over last year with the percent changes in its net income and operating assets. Major disparities are worth a look.

Reading financial statements is the best way to get acquainted with the financial structure of a business that you're thinking of investing in. Don't worry too much about the accounting methods used by public companies. For privately owned companies, however, you should keep an eye on the major accounting policies of the business and how these accounting methods affect reported earnings and asset values.

Disclosure in financial statements leaves a lot to be desired. Don't look for a road map of the profit strategy of a business in its financial reports. Keep in mind that the total value of a business is not to be found in its balance sheet. Until an actual buyer of a business makes a serious offer, there is no particular reason to determine the value of the business as a going concern. Value depends mainly on the past earnings record of the business as forecast into the future.

The main message of this final chapter is to be prudent and careful in making decisions based on financial statements. Many investors and managers don't seem to be aware of the limitations of financial statements. Used intelligently, financial reports are the indispensable starting point for making investment and lending decisions. I hope my book helps you make better decisions. Good luck, and be careful out there.

INDEX